A Garland Series

The English Stage
Attack and Defense 1577 - 1730

A collection of 90 important works
reprinted in photo-facsimile in 50 volumes

edited by
Arthur Freeman
Boston University

The Usefulness
of the Stage

by

John Dennis

with a preface
for the Garland Edition by

Arthur Freeman

Garland Publishing, Inc., New York & London

1972

Library of Congress Cataloging in Publication Data

Dennis, John, 1657-1734.
    The usefulness of the stage.

    (The English stage: attack and defense, 1577-1730)
    Reprint of the 1698 ed.
    "Wing D1046."
    1. Collier, Jeremy, 1650-1726. A short view of the
immorality and profaneness of the English stage.
2. Theater--Moral and religious aspects. 3. Theater--
England. I. Title. II. Series.
PN2047.C62D4 1972   792'.013   71-170441
ISBN 0-8240-0609-7

Preface

Edward Niles Hooker, The Critical Works of John Dennis *(two vols., Baltimore, 1939-1943), has edited the text of this "first comprehensive reply to Collier" (I, 146-93) and commented exhaustively upon it (I, 466-79) placing Dennis's unanswered remarks in an historical and critical perspective which remains wholly persuasive. Hooker's text is basically that of the present original edition, but with errata and a few typographical slips silently corrected, some punctuation modernized, and much bewilderingly arbitrary alteration of capitalization, font, and even spelling (eight added upper-case initial letters and two unnecessary mis-spellings in the last paragraph of the book alone, for example).*

Our reprint is prepared from British Museum 641.e.4, collating $A^4 B-K^8$ (vertical chainlines), with Errata on the verso of K8; in some copies $K8^v$ is blank. The Usefulness of the Stage *was first advertised in the 4-7 June 1698 issue of* The Post Man, *a few days only before Vanbrugh's* Short

5

PREFACE

Vindication. *It was reprinted in the undated compilation called* Miscellaneous Tracts *(1725 in Lowe-Arnott-Robinson; c. 1727 teste Hooker), and in a "mutilated" or reduced version of 1738 (two issues).*

Lowe-Arnott-Robinson 308; Hooker 7; Wing D 1046.

July, 1972   A. F.

THE
USEFULNESS
OF THE
STAGE,

To the Happiness of
Mankind.
To Government, and
To Religion.

Occasioned by a late Book,
written by *Jeremy Collier*, M. A.

By Mr. *DENNIS*.

LONDON,
Printed for *Rich. Parker* at the *Unicorn* under
the Piazza of the *Royal Exchange.* 1698.

INTRODUCTION.

THe beſt things here below, are liable to be corrupted, and the better things are in their own natures, the more miſchievous are they if corrupted. For that which is ſuperlatively good in it ſelf can be corrupted by nothing but extraordinary malice. Since then the Stage is acknowledg'd by its greateſt adverſaries to be in itſelf good, and inſtrumental to the inſtruction of mankind, nothing can be more unreaſonable than to exhort people to ruin it inſtead of reforming it, ſince at that rate we muſt think of aboliſhing much more important eſtabliſhments. Yet that is apparently the deſign of Mr *Collier*'s Book, tho his malice infinitely ſurpaſſing his ability, as it certainly does, whatever ſome people may think of him, his performance is ſomewhat awkward. For in the Intro-

A 2   duction

duction to his Book he gives you reasons why the Stage in general ought to
be commended; in the first Chapters of
his Book he pretends to shew cause
why the *English* Stage ought to be reform'd, and in the sixth and last Chapter
he pretends to prove by Authority that
no Stage ought to be allow'd. In the
beginning of his Book he produces his
own reasons why the Stage reform'd
ought to be encourag'd, and in the end
of the same Book he brings other mens
opinions to shew that every Stage ought
to be abolish'd; and so endeavours to
ruine his own Reasons by a long scroll
of other peoples Authorities, which is
certainly a pleasant condescension;
but such is the fantastick humility of
pedantick pride. And yet Mr *Collier*
is very right and very sincere in his
Reasons, and very wrong and very
corrupt in his Authorities. As if he
were so great an enemy to the truth,
that he would suborn the very dead to
destroy the force of what he himself
had asserted.

If Mr *Collier* had only attack'd the
Corruptions of the Stage, for my own
part I should have been so far from
blaming

blaming him, that I should have pub-
lickly return'd him my thanks: For the
abuses are so great, that there is a necessity for the reforming them; not
that I think that with all its corruptions
the Stage has debauch'd the people: I am fully convinc'd it has not,
and I believe I have said enough in the
following treatise to convince the Reader of it.   But this is certain, that the
corruptions of the Stage hinder its effi-
cacy in the reformation of manners.
For, besides that Vice is contrary to
Virtue, it renders the Stage little and
contemptible; for nothing but Virtue
can make any thing awful and truly
great, and nothing but what is awful
and truly great can be universally re-
spected, and by that means in a condition to influence the minds of the people.   For this reason, as I said above,
if Mr *Collier* had only attack'd the licentiousness of the Stage, in so fair a
manner as he ought to have done it, I
had return'd him my thanks, but when
I found by his last Chapter, that his design was against the Stage it self, I thought
I could not spend a month more use-
fully, than in the vindication of it.

My

My bufinefs therefore is a vindication
of the Stage, and not of the Corruptions or the abufes of it. And therefore
I have no further meddled with Mr.
Collier's Book, than as I have had occafion to fhew, that he has endeavour'd
to make fome things pafs for abufes, either of the Stage in general, or of the
Englifh Stage particularly, which are fo
far from being abufes, that they may be
accounted excellences.

This little Treatife was conceiv'd,
difpos'd, tranfcrib'd and printed in a
month; and tho on that very account
it may not be wholly free from error,
yet this I can affure the Reader, that
I have induftrioufly endeavour'd not
to err, tho I verily believe that Mr *Collier* induftrioufly endeavour'd to err,
as far as he thought it might be confift-
ent with the deceiving of others.

The method that I have ufed has
been this: I have endeavoured to fhew
that the Stage in general is ufeful to the
happinefs of Mankind, to the welfare
of Government, and the advancement of
Religion : And under the head of Government I have endeavour'd to prove,
that the Stage does not encourage Revenge,

venge, as Mr *Collier* afferts in his laft
Chapter; and that by encouraging
Pride, which is another thing that he
charges upon it, it provides for the
happinefs of particular men, and the
publick. I have endeavour'd to fhew
too, in defence of the *English*
Stage, that it is to be commended for its
impartiality, and in exempting no degree or order of men from cenfure.

I faw very well that there was no
proceeding any farther in the vindication of it: For no man can make any
reafonable defence, either for the immorality or the immodefty, or the
unneceffary wanton prophanenefs,
which are too juftly charg'd upon it.
But for the particular Gentlemen which
Mr *Collier* has attack'd in fome particular paffages, which he has induftrioufly
cull'd from their writings, I could make
a very good defence for feveral of 'em,
if I were not fatisfied that they were
abler to defend themfelves.

He has treated them indeed with
the laft difdain, and the laft contempt,
not confidering, that by doing it, he
has treated all at the fame rate, who
profefs an efteem for them, that is, all
the

the Town. He has given them some language which muſt be reſented by all who profeſs Humanity.

For, Mr *Collier* is ſo far from having ſhown in his Book, either the meekneſs of a true Chriſtian, or the humility of an exemplary Paſtor, that he has neither the reaſoning of a man of ſenſe in it, nor the ſtyle of a polite man, nor the ſincerity of an honeſt man, nor the humanity of a Gentleman, or a man of Letters.

THE

THE
USEFULNESS
OF THE
STAGE.

CHAP. I.

That the Stage is instrumental to the Happiness of Mankind.

Nothing can more strongly recommend any thing to us, than the assuring us, that it will improve our happiness. For the chief end

B   *and*

and defign of man is to make himfelf happy. Tis what he conftantly has in his eye, and in order to which, he takes every ftep that he makes: In whatever he does or he does not, he defigns to improve or maintain his happinefs. And 'tis by this univerfal principle, that God maintains the harmony, and order, and quiet of the reafonable World. It had indeed been an inconfiftency in providence, to have made a thinking and reafoning Creature, that had been indifferent as to mifery and happinefs; for God had made fuch a one only to difturb the reft, and confequently had acted againft his own defign.

If then I can fay enough to convince the Reader, that the Stage is inftrumental to the happinefs of Mankind, and to his own by confequence, it is evident that I need fay no more to make him efpoufe its interest.

I fhall proceed then to the proving thefe two things..

Firft, That the Stage is inftrumental to the happinefs of Mankind in general.

Secondly, That it is more particularly inftrumental to the happinefs of *Englifhmen*.

The

The Stage is inſtrumental to the happineſs of Mankind in general. And here it will be neceſſary to declare what is meant by happineſs, and to proceed upon that.

By happineſs then, I never could underſtand any thing elſe but pleaſure; for I never could have any notion of happineſs, that did not agree with pleaſure, or any notion of pleaſure, that did not agree with happineſs. I could never poſſibly conceive how any one can be happy without being pleas'd, or pleas'd without being happy. 'Tis univerſally acknowledg'd by Mankind, that happineſs conſiſts in pleaſure, which is evident from this, that whatever a man does, whether in ſpiritual or temporal affairs, whether in matters of profit or diverſion, pleaſure is at leaſt the chief and the final motive to it, if it is not the immediate one. And providence ſeems to have ſufficiently declar'd, that pleaſure was intended for our Spring and Fountain of Action, when it made it the incentive to thoſe very acts, by which we propagate our kind and preſerve our ſelves. As if Self-love without pleaſure were inſufficient for

either;

either ; for as I my self have know several, who have chosen rather to dye,
than to go through tedious courses of
Physick ; so I make no doubt, but several would have taken the same reso-
lution, rather than have supported life
by a perpetual course of eating, which
had differ'd in nothing from a course
of Physick, if eating and pleasure had
not been things inseparable. Now as 'tis
pleasure that obliges man to perserve
himself, it is the very same that has sometimes the force to prevail upon him to his
own destruction. For as Monsieur *Pascal*
observes, the very men who hang, and
who drown themselves are instigated by
the secret pleasure, which they have
from the thought that they shall be
freed from pain.

Since therefore man, in every thing
that he does proposes pleasure to himself, it follows, that in pleasure consists
his happiness. But tho he always proposes it, he very often falls short of it,
For pleasure is not in his own power,
since if it were, it would follow from
thence, that happiness were in his
power. The want of which has been
always the complaint of men, both sacred

cred and secular, in all Ages, in all Countries, and in all Conditions. *Man that is born of a woman is but of few days, and full of trouble,* says *Job* Chap. 14. Verse 1. Of the same nature are the two complaints of *Horace*, which are so fine, and so poetical, and so becoming of the best antiquity.

Scandit æratas vitiosa naves
Curæ, nec turmas equitum & relinquit
Oçior Cervis, & agente Nimbos
Ocyor Euro,

Hor. Ode
Lib. 2.

And that other, in the first Ode of the third Book.

Timor & minæ
Scandunt eodem quo Dominus, neque
Decedit ærata triremi, &
Post equitem sedit atra cura.

In short, they who have made the most reflections on it, have been the most satisfy'd of it, and above all Philosophers; who, by the voluminous instructions, by the laborious directions which they have left to posterity, have declar'd themselves sensible,

B 3   that

that to be happy is a very difficult thing.

And the reason why they of all men have always found it so difficult is, because they always propounded to owe their happiness to reason, tho one would think, that experience might have convinc'd them of the folly of such a design, because they had seen that the most thinking and the most reasonable, had always most complain'd.

For reason may often afflict us, and make us miserable, by setting our impotence or our guilt before us; but that which it generally does, is the maintaining us in a languishing state of indifference, which perhaps is more remov'd from pleasure, than that is from affliction, and which may be said to be the ordinary state of men.

It is plain then, that reason by maintaining us in that state, is an impediment to our pleasure, which is our happiness. For to be pleas'd a man must come out of his ordinary state; now nothing in this life can bring him out of it but passion alone, which Reason pretends to combat.

No-

Nothing but paffion in effect can pleafe us, which every one may know by experience : For when any man is pleas'd, he may find by reflection that at the fame time he is mov'd. The pleafure that any man meets with ofteneft is the pleafure of Sence. Let any one examine himfelf in that, and he will find that the pleafure is owing to paffion ; for the pleafure vanifhes with the defire, and is fucceeded by loathing, which is a fort of grief.

Since nothing but pleafure can make us happy, it follows that to be very happy, we muft be much pleas'd ; and fince nothing but paffion can pleafe us, it follows that to be very much pleas'd we muft be very much mov'd ; this needs no proof, or if it did, experience would be a very convincing one; fince any one may find when he has a great deal of pleafure that he is extremely mov'd.

And that very height and fulnefs of pleafure which we are promis'd in another life, muft, we are told, proceed from paffion, or fomething which refembles paffion. At leaft no man has fo much as pretended that it will be

B 4 the

the result of Reason.   For we shall then
be deliver'd from these mortal Organs,
and Reason shall then be no more.   We
shall then no more have occasion from
premisses to draw conclusions, and a
long train of consequences; for, becoming all spirit and all knowledge, we
shall see things as they are : We shall
lead the glorious life of Angels, a life
exalted above all Reason, a life consisting of Extasie and Intelligence.

Thus is it plain that the happiness
both of this life and the other is owing to
passion, and not to reason.   But tho
we can never be happy by the force of
Reason, yet while we are in this life
we cannot possibly be happy without
it, or against it.   For since man is by
his nature a reasonable creature , to
suppose man happy against Reason, is
to suppose him happy against Nature,
which is absurd and monstrous.   We
have shewn, that a man must be pleas'd
to be happy, and must be mov'd to be
pleas'd ; and that to please him to a
height, you must move him in propor-
tion: But then the passions must be
rais'd after such a manner as to take
reason along with them.   If reason is
                                    quite

quite overcome, the pleasure is neither long, nor sincere, nor safe. For how many that have been transported beyond their reason, have never more recover'd it. If reason resists, a mans breast becomes the seat of Civil War, and the Combat makes him miserable. For these passions, which are in their natures so very troublesome, are only so because their motions are always contrary to the motion of the will; as grief, sorrow, shame and jealousie. And that which makes some passions in their natures pleasant, is because they move with the will, as love, joy, pity, hope, terror, and sometimes anger. But this is certain, that no passion can move in these a full consent with the will, unless at the same time it be approv'd of by the understanding. And no passion can be allow'd of by the understanding, that is not rais'd by its true springs, and augmented by its just degrees. Now in the world it is so very rare to have our passions thus rais'd, and so improv'd, that that is the reason why we are so seldom throughly and sincerely pleas'd. But in the Drama the passions are false and abominable,

ble, unless they are mov'd by their
true springs, and rais'd by their just
degrees. Thus are they mov'd, thus
are they rais'd in every well writ Tragedy, till they come to as great a height
as reason can very well bear. Besides,
the very motion has a tendency to the
subjecting them to reason, and the very
raising purges and moderates them.
So that the passions are seldom any
where so pleasing, and no where so
safe as they are in Tragedy. Thus
have I shown, that to be happy is to
be pleas'd, and that to be pleas'd is to
be mov'd in such a manner as is allow'd
of by Reason; I have shown too that
Tragedy moves us thus, and consequently pleases us, and conseqeuntly makes us
happy. Which was the thing to he prov'd.

CHAP.

CHAP. II.

*That the Stage is more parti-
cularly instrumental to the
happiness of* English *men.*

WE have fhown in the former
Chapter, that all happinefs con-
fifts in pleafure, and that all pleafure
proceeds from paffion ; but that paffion to produce pleafure, muft be rais'd
after fuch a manner, as to move in con-
fent with the will, and confequently
to be allow'd of by the underftanding,
upon which we took an occafion to
fhew, that thinking and reafoning people as Philofophers, and the like,
have made moft complaints of the mifery of humane life, becaufe they have
endeavour'd to deduce their happinefs
from reafon, and not from paffion.
But another reafon may be given, and
that is, that fuch people, by reafon of
the

the exactness or moroseness of their judgments, are too scrupulous in the allowance of the passions, from whence it proceeds, that things very rarely happen in life, to raise their passions in such a manner, as to approve them to their understandings, and consequently to make them move in consent with their wills. From whence it proceeds, that splenatick persons are so very unhappy, and so much harder to be pleas'd than others, which is every day confirm'd by experience. Indeed 'tis observ'd every day in splenatick people, that their passions move for the most part, with a contrary motion to that of their wills, and so afflict them them instead of delighting them. Now there is no Nation in *Europe*, as has been observ'd above a thousand times, that is so generally addicted to the Spleen as the *English*. And which is apparent to any observer, from the reigning distemper of the Clime, which is inseparable from the Spleen; from that gloomy and sullen temper, which is generally spread through the Nation: from that natural discontentedness which makes us so uneasie to one another,

ther, becaufe we are fo uneafie to our felves ; and laftly, from our jealoufies and fufpicions, which makes us fo uneafie to our felves, and to one another, and have fo often made us dangerous to the Government, and by confequence to our felves. Now the *Englifh* being more fplenatick than other people, and confequently more thoughtful and more reflecting, and therefore more fcrupulous in allowing their paffions, and confequently things feldom hapning in life to move their paffions fo agreeably to their reafons, as to entertain and pleafe them ; and there being no true and fincere pleafure unlefs thefe paffions are thus mov'd, nor any happinefs without pleafure; it follows, that the *Englifh* to be happy, have more need than other people of fomething that will raife their paffions in fuch a manner, as fhall be agreeable to their reafons, and that by confequence they have more need of the Drama.

CHAP.

CHAP. III.

The Objections from Reason answer'd.

BUt now we proceed to answer Objections, and to shew that we design to use Mr *Collier* with all the fairness imaginable; I shall not only endeavour to answer all that may be objected from Mr. *Collier's* Book; against what I have said in the foregoing Chapters in the behalf of the Stage; I say, I shall not only endeavour to answer this, after I have propounded it in the most forcible manner in which it can be urg'd, but I shall make it my business to reply to all that has been objected by other adversaries, or that I can foresee may be hereafter objected.

The objections then against what I have said in Defence of the Stage in the foregoing Chapters, are or may be of three sorts.   **First,**

Firſt, Objections from Reaſon.
Secondly, From Authority, and
Thirdly, From Religion.

Firſt then, I ſhall endeavour to anſwer what may be objected from
Reaſon, *viz.* That tho it ſhould be
granted that the Theatre makes people happy for the preſent, yet it afterwards infallibly makes them miſerable:
Firſt, by nouriſhing and fomenting their
paſſions; and ſecondly, by indulging
their vices, and making them Liber-
tines: And that 'tis neither the part of
a prudent man, nor a good Chriſtian,
to make choice of ſuch a momentary
delight, as will be follow'd by ſo much
affliction.

And firſt, ſay the Adverſaries of the
Stage, the Drama tends to the making
of people unhappy, becauſe it nouriſhes
and foments thoſe paſſions, that occaſion the follies and imprudencies from
whence come all their misfortunes:
And

Firſt, It indulges Terror and Pity,
and the reſt of the paſſions.

Se-

Secondly, It not only indulges Love where it is, but creates it where it is not.

First then, say they, it indulges Terror, Pity, and the rest of the passions. For, says a certain *French* Gentleman, who is famous for Criticism, that purgation which *Aristotle* mentions is meerly chimerical; the more the passions in any one are mov'd, the more obnoxious they are to be mov'd, and the more unruly they grow.

But, by Monsieur *De St. Evremont's* favour, this is not only to contradict *Aristotle,* but every mans daily experience. For every man finds, and every man of sense particularly, that the longer he frequents Plays the harder he is to be pleas'd, that is, the harder he is to be mov'd; and when any man of judgment, who has a long time frequented Plays, happens to be very much touch'd by a Scene, we may conclude that that Scene is very well writ, both for nature and art.

And indeed, if people who have a long time frequented Plays are so hard to be mov'd to compassion, that a Poet is oblig'd so to contrive his incidents

and

and his Characters, that the last shall
be most deplorable, and the first most
proper to move compassion; may it not
be very well suppos'd, that such a one
will not be over obnoxious to feel too
much compassion upon the view of calamities, which happen every day in the
world, when they and the persons to
whom they happen, may not so much
as once in an Age, have all the qualifications that are requir'd extreamly to
touch him.

But, Secondly, whereas it is urg'd,
that the Drama and particularly Tragedy, manifestly indulges Love where
it is, and creates it where it is not. To
this I answer. That the Love which is
shewn in a Tragedy is lawful and regular, or it is not. If it is not, why
then in a Play, which is writ as it should
be (for I pretend not to defend the
errours or corruptions of the Stage) it
is shewn unfortunate in the Catastro-
phe, which is sufficient to make an Audience averse from engaging in the
excesses of that passion. But if the
Love that is shewn is lawful and regular, nothing makes a man happier than
that passion. I speak ev'n of that i m-
C   mediate

mediate pleasure which attends the passion itself. And as it certainly makes him happy for the present, so there is no passion which puts a man upon things that make him happier for the future. For as people have for the most part a very high opinion of the belov'd object, it makes them endeavour to become worthy of it, and to encrease in knowledge and virtue; and not only frequently reclaims them from some grosser pleasures, of which they were fond before, but breeds in them an utter detestation of some unnatural vices, which have been so much in use in *England*, for these last thirty years.

But now we come to the second pretended Reason, why the Drama tends to the making of men unhappy, and that is, say the Adversaries of the Stage, because it encourages and indulges their vices. To which we answer; that the Drama, and particulary Tragedy, in its purity, is so far from having that effect, that it must of necessity make men virtuous; First, because it moderates the passions, whose excesses cause their vices; Secondly, because it instructs them in their duties, both by its fable
and

and by its sentences. But here they start an objection, which some imagin a strong one, which is, That the Nation has been more corrupted since the establishment of the Drama, upon the restoration, than ever it was before. To which I answer.

First, That that corruption of manners, tho it should be granted to proceed from the Stage, can yet only proceed from the licentious abuses of it, which no man pretends to defend. But,

Secondly, We affirm that this corruption of manners, cannot be reasonably said to proceed, no not even from those palpable abuses of the Stage, which we will not pretend to vindicate.

First, For if the corruption of manners proceeded from the abuses of the Stage, how comes it to pass that we never heard any complaint of the like corruption of manners before the restoration of *Charles* the Second, since it is plain from Mr *Collier*'s Book, that the Drama flourish'd in the Reign of King *James* I. and flourish'd with the like licentiousness. But,

Secondly, if this general corruption
of manners is to be attributed to the
abuses of the Stage, from hence it will
follow, that there should be the greatest corruption of manners where the
Theatres are most frequented, or most
licentious, which is not true: for in
France the Theatres are less licentious
than ours, and yet the corruption of
manners is there as great, if you only
except our drinking, which, as I shall
prove anon, can never proceed from
any encouragement of the Stage. In
Germany and in *Italy* the Theatres are
less frequented: for in *Italy* they seldom
have Plays unless in the Carnival, and
in most of the little *German* Soveraignties, they have not constant Theatres.
And yet in *Germany* they drink more,
and in *Italy* they are more intemperate
in the use of women and unnatural
vices.

But Thirdly, The corruption of
manners upon the restoration, appear'd
with all the fury of Libertinism, even
before the Play House was re-establisht
and long before it could have any influence on manners, so that another cause
of that corruption is to be enquir'd after,
                                              than

than the re-establishment of the Drama, and that can be nothing but that beastly reformation, which in the time of the late Civil Wars, was begun at the Tail instead of the Head and the Heart; and which opprest and persecuted mens inclinations, instead of correcting and converting them, which afterwards broke out with the same violence, that a raging fire does upon its first getting vent. And that which gave it so licentious a vent was, not only the permission, but the example of the Court, which for the most part was just arriv'd from abroad with the King, where it had endeavour'd by foreign corruption to sweeten, or at least to soften adversity, and having sojourn'd for a considerable time, both at *Paris* and in the *Low Countries*, united the spirit of the *French* Whoring, to the fury of the *Dutch* Drinking. So that the Poets who writ immediately after the restoration, were obliged to humour the deprav'd tastes of their Audience. For as an impenitent Sinner that should be immediately transported to Heaven, would be incapable of partaking of the happiness of the place, because his in-

C 3   cli-

clinations and affections would not be
prepar'd for it, so if the Poets of these
times had writ in a manner purely instructive, without any mixture of lewdness, the Appetites of the Audience
were so far debauch'd, that they would
have judg'd the entertainment insipid,
so that the spirit of Libertinism which
came in with the Court, and for which
the people were so well prepar'd by
the sham-reformation of manners,
caus'd the lewdness of their Plays, and
not the lewdness of Plays the spirit of
Libertinism.   For 'tis ridiculous to assign a cause of so long a standing to
so new, so sudden, and so extraordinary an effect, when we may assign a cause
so new, so probable, and unheard of
before, as the inclinations of the people, returning with violence to their
natural bent, upon the encouragement
and example of a Court, that was
come home with all the corruptions
of a foreign Luxury ; so that the sham-
reformation being in a great measure
the cause of that spirit of Libertinism,
which with so much fury came in with
King *Charles* the Second, and the put-
ting down the Play House being part
of

of that reformation, 'tis evident that the Corruption of the Nation is so far from proceeding from the Play-house, that it partly proceeds from having no Plays at all.

Fourthly, That the Corruption of Manners is not to be attributed to the licentiousness of the Drama, may appear from the consideration of the reigning vices, I mean those moral vices which have more immediate influence upon mens conduct, and consequently upon their happiness. And those are chiefly four.

1. The love of Women.
2. Drinking.
3. Gaming.
4. Unnatural sins.

For drinking and gaming, their excesses cannot be reasonably charg'd upon the Stage, for the following Reasons.

First, Because it cannot possibly be conceiv'd, that so reasonable a diversion as the Drama, can encourage or incline men to so unreasonable a

C 4   one

one as gaming, or so brutal a one as drunkenness.

Secondly, Because these two vices have been made odious and ridiculous by our Plays, instead of being shewn agreeable. As for Drunkenness, to shew the sinner is sufficient to discredit the vice ; for a Drunkard of necessity always appears either odious or ridiculous. And for a Gamester, I never knew any one shewn in a Play, but either as a Fool or a Rascal.

Thirdly, Because those two vices flourish in places that are too remote, and in persons that are too abject to be encourag'd or influenc'd by the Stage. There is drinking and gaming in the furthest North and the furthest West, among Peasants, as well as among Dukes and Peers. But here perhaps some visionary Zealot will urge, that these two vices, even these remote places, and these abject persons proceed from the influence of that irreligion, which is caus'd by the corruptions of the Stage, and will with as much reason and as much modesty deduce the lewdness which is transacted in the Tin mines, in *Cornwal*, and in the Coal-pits of *Newcastle*, from the daily a-
bominations

bominations of the Pits of the two Play-
houfes, as he would derive the brutality
of the high *Dutch* Drinking, from the
prophaneneſs of our *Engliſh* Drama.

But what will he ſay then to thoſe
Gentlemen, who neither are ſuppos'd to
go to our Theatres, nor to converſe
much with thoſe who do, nor to be
liable to be corrupted by them; what
will they ſay to theſe Gentlemen, if they
can be prov'd to have a confiderable
ſhare of the two fore-mention'd vices?
What can they anſwer? For it would be
ridiculouſly abſurd to reply, that the
Clergy are corrupted by the Laity, whom
it is their buſineſs to convert. But here
I think my ſelf oblig'd to declare, that I
by no means deſign this as a reflection
upon the Church of *England*, who I am
ſatisfy'd may more juſtly boaſt of its Clergy,
than any other Church whatſoever; a
Clergy that are equally illuſtrious for their
Piety and for their Learning, yet may I
venture to affirm, that there are ſome a-
mong them, who can never be ſuppos'd
to have been corrupted by Play-houſes,
who yet turn up a Bottle oftner than they
do an Hour-glaſs, who box about a pair
of Tables with more fervour than they
do

do their Cushions, contemplate a pair of
Dice more frequently than the Fathers or
Councels, and meditate and depend upon Hazard, more than they do upon Providence.

And as for that unnatural sin, which
is another growing vice of the Age,
it would be monstrous to urge that it
is in the least encourag'd by the Stage,
for it is either never mention'd there,
or mention'd with the last detestation.

And now lastly, for the Love of
Women, fomented by the Corruption,
and not by the genuine Art of the
Stage; tho the augmenting and nou-
rishing it cannot be defended, yet it
may be in some measure excus'd.

1. Because it has more of Nature,
and consequently more Temptation,
and consequently less Malice, than the
preceding three, which the Drama
does not encourage.

2. Because it has a check upon the
other Vices, and peculiarly upon that
unnatural sin, in the restraining of
which the happiness of mankind is in
so evident a manner concern'd.

So that of the four moral reigning vices, the Stage encourages but one, which, as it has been prov'd to be the leaft of them all, fo is it the leaft contageous, and the leaft univerfal. For in the Country, Fornication and Adultery are feldom heard of, whereas Drunkennefs rages in almoft every houfe there : From all which it appears, how very unreafonable it is, to charge the lewdnefs of the times upon the Stage, when it is evident, that of the four reigning moral vices, the Stage encourages but one, and that the leaft of the four, and the leaft univerfal, and a vice which has a check upon the other three, and particularly upon that amongft them, which is moft oppofite and moft deftructive to the happinefs of mankind.

C A A P.

CHAP. IV.

The Objections from Authority answer'd.

IN the next place we come to answer the objections which Mr *Collier* has brought from Authority. The Authorities which he has produc'd are indeed very numerous, yet only four of them can be reduc'd under this head, without running into confusion, two Poets and two Philosophers.

The Poets are *Ovid* and Mr. *Wycherley*; the Philosophers, *Plutarch* and *Seneca*.

The first of them is *Ovid*, in his Book *De Arte Amandi*, and in his Book *De Remedio Amoris*. We have already answer'd the last in the preceding Chapter, and shall now say something to the first. The passage is this :

Sed

Sed Tu præcipue Curvis Venare Theatris
  Hæc loca sunt votis Fertiliora tuis.
Illic invenies quod ames, quod Ludere possis
  Quodꝗ semel Tangas quodꝗ Tenere velis.

From whence Mr *Collier* makes this
shrewd Remark, that the Theatre is
the properest place in the world to
meet, or to find a Mistress, and that
several people go thither on purpose.
In answer to this, I desire the Reader
to peruse the Verses which precede.

Nec Fuge niliginæ Memphitica Templa Ju-
                                   vencæ
  Multas illa facit quod fuit illa Jovi.

And have we not here a merry person?
who brings an Authority against going
to Theatres, which is as direct against
going to Church? Nay, and upon the
very same account too. But the Poet
speaks here of a Heathen Temple, says
Mr *Collier.* Well, and so he does of a
Heathen Theatre. But what he says
of the *Roman* Theatre is exactly applicable to ours. And what Reply can be
made to that, says Mr *Collier*? What?
                              Why

Why I wish to God that no Reply
could be made to it. But besides, if
several people go to our Theatres purposely to meet, or to find out a Mistress, I think it is plain that if there
were no Theatres, they wou'd go to
other places : Especially since, as we
hinted above, when the Theatres are
shut, they frequent other Assemblies
upon the same designs. But tho some
people go to the Theatre to meet their
Mistresses, yet it is evident that most
go to see the Play, who, if they could
not have that diversion, would not
improbably go to other places with far
worse intentions.

The next who is produc'd against
the Stage is Mr *Wycherley*, much, I dare
say, against the assent either of his will
or his understanding. But only for a
jest in that admirable Epistle, which is
prefix'd to the *Plain Dealer*. However, even that jest. let it be never so
much o're-strain'd, can never be brought
to convince us of any thing but the
abuses of the Theatre; which I do not
pretend to defend ; and I thought Mr
Wycherley had more than made amends
for it, by exposing Adultery, and making

king it the immediate cause of *Olivia's* misfortune, in that excellent Play, which is a most instructive and a most noble Satyr, upon the hyprocrisie and villany of Mankind.

Mr *Wycherley* being indeed almost the only man alive, who has made Comedy instructive in its Fable; almost all the rest being contented to instruct by their characters. But what Mr *Collier* has said of Mr *Wycherley* is sufficient to shew us what Candour, nay, and what Justice we are to expect from this censurer of the Stage. For in giving Mr *Wycherley's* Character, he has shewn himself invidious and detracting even in his commendation. For the best thing that he can afford to say of the greatest of our Comick Wits, is, that he is a man of good sense. Which puts me in mind of a Father in *France* overhearing his Son saying of the Mareschal de *Turenne, Ma foy, Je trouve Monsieur de Turenne an Joly Homme: Et vous mon fits,* replys the Father, *je vous trouve un joly sot de parler ainsi, Du plus grand Homme que la France a parte.* How unworthy was it to commend Mr *Wycherley* for a thing, which, tho

cer-

certainly he has in a very great degree, yet is common to him with a thousand more; and to take no notice of those extraordinary qualities which are peculiar to him alone, his Wit, his Penetration, his Satyr, his Art, his Characters, and above all, that incomparable Vivacity, by which he has happily equall'd the Ancients, and surpass'd the Moderns?

But now let us pass to the Philosophers, I mean the Philosophers who were not Poets; for no man can be a good Poet who is not a Philosopher. He has cited *Plutarch* in four several places in his *Symposiacum*; his Book *De Audiendis Poetis*; his Treatise *De gloria Atheniensium*; and his *Laconick Institutions*: For the two last we shall say nothing to them, till we come to speak of government. In the two first Mr *Collier* makes *Plutarch* say, that Plays are dangerous to corrupt young people, and therefore Stage-poetry, when it grows too hardy, and licentious, ought to be check'd. But I make no doubt but to make it appear, that Mr *Collier* has been guilty of three things in this very action, which are unworthy the Candour of a Gentleman, or of a man of
Letters.

Lettets. First, he has brought an Authority, which can only convince us that this Philosopher did not approve of the licentiousness of the Stage, which licentiousness we by no means design to defend : such an Authority, I say, he has brought in a Chapter, design'd to shew that the Ancients disapprov'd of Plays, and the Stage in general. Secondly, he has made use of the Authority of *Plutarch* against the Stage, whereas that Philosopher has said infinitely more in its behalf, than he has against it. Thirdly, he has from two tracts of *Plutarch* slurr'd one citation upon us in the way of an argument, which is very unlike the reasoning of that Philosopher. For in the first part of the Enthyme, he makes *Plutarch* damn the Stage, and the Drama in general ; and in the second conclude against them in particular. For Plays, says he, that is, all Plays, are dangerous to corrupt young people, and therefore some Plays ought to be check'd. And why does Mr *Collier* make the Philosopher argue after this Jesuitical manner, when it is plain to any Reader, that has but common apprehension, that

since

since in the second part of the *Euthy-mene* , *Plutarch* condemn'd only some particular Plays; he only said in the first part of it, that some particular Plays were dangerous. But let us proceed to *Seneca*. And since it highly concerns us to give a full and satisfactory account of what is objected from him, let us cite him at length, as Mr *Collier* translates him. Seneca *complains heartily of the extravagance and debauchery of the Age : And how forward people were to improve in that which was naught. That scarce any body would apply themselves to the study of Nature and Morality, unless when the Play-house was shut, or the weather foul. That there was no body to teach Philosophy, because there was no body to learn it. But that the Stage had nurseries, and company enough. This misapplication of Time and Fancy, made Knowledge in so ill a condition. This was the cause the Hints of Antiquity were no better pursued; that some inventions were sunk, and that some inventions grew downwards, rather than otherwise.* To which I answer, First, that it is not likely that *Seneca* should condemn the Drama and the Stage in general, since

it

it is so notoriously known that he writ Plays himself. Secondly, that by what he says it is evident that he declaims only against the abuses of the Theatre; and those such abuses as have no relation to ours; as for example, the passing whole days together in the Theatre, which the *Romans* oftentimes did. Thirdly, that if Mr *Collier* would infer from hence, that our Theatres are hindrances to the advancement of Learning, we have nothing to do but affirm what all the world must consent to, that Learning is now at a greater height than ever it was known in *England*.

What we have said is sufficient to confound Mr *Collier*, but we will not be contented with that; for here we triumph, here we insult, here we have a just occasion to shew the admirable advantage of the Stage to Letters, and the incomparable excellency of the Drama, and in a more peculiar manner of Tragedy, which seems purposely form'd and design'd for the raising the mind, and firing it to that noble emulation, which is so absolutely necessary for the improvement of Arts. This is a truth which is confirm'd by the experience of all Nations, of all Ages. For whether we look upon the Ancients or Moderns, whether we consider the *Athenians* or *Romans*, or the *French* or our selves, we shall find that Arts and Sciences have for the most part begun, but all of them at least begun to prosper with the Stage, and that as they have flourish'd, they have at last declin'd with it. And this we may affirm, not only of the the more human Arts, Poetry, History, Eloquence, of which the Theatre is certainly the best School in the world; the School that form'd in a great measure those prodigious Disciples, *Cicero* and *Demosthenes*, but we may truly assert it of all other sorts of Learning.

For before *Thespis* appear'd in *Attica*, and reduc'd the Drama to some sort of form, which had nothing but confusion before him, they had neither Author nor Knowledge amongst them, that could be esteem'd by posterity: That little knowledge which they had of Nature is to us ridiculous. For Moral Philosophy, they had no such thing, nor Orator nor Historian. But as soon as

after

after *Thespis* their Theatre began to flourish, all their extraordinary men, in all these sorts, appear'd almost together. Not only those who adorn'd the Stage, as *Æschylus, Euripides*, and the divine *Sophocles* ; but those Orators, Philosophers and Historians, who have since been the wonders of all posterity, *Socrates, Plato, Xenophon, Aristotle, Pericles, Thucydides, Demosthenes, Æschines* ; and of all their famous Authors who have descended to us, there was not one that I can think of, but who was alive between the first appearing of *Thespis*, and the death of *Sophocles.* And be it said in a more particular manner for the honour of the Stage, that they had no such thing as Moral Philosophy before the Drama flourish'd. *Socrates* was the first, who out of their Theatre began to form their manners. And be it said, to the immortal honour of Tragedy, that the first and greatest of all the Moral Philosophers, not only frequented their Theatres, but was employ'd in writing Tragedies.

And as among the *Athenians*, Eloquence, History, and Philosophy, I

speak

speak of the moral, which is the only
solid certain Philosophy, appear'd and
flourish'd upon the flourishing of the
Stage, so with the Stage they at last
declin'd, for not one of their famous
writers has descended to us, who liv'd
after the Drama was come to perfection,
that is, after the full establishment of
the new Comedy.

As Dramatick Poetry was the first
kind of writing that appear'd among
the *Athenians*, so I defy the most skil-
ful man in antiquity, to name so much
as one Author among the *Romans* till
Dramatick Poetry appear'd at *Rome*,
introduc'd by *Livius Andronicus*, above
five hundred years after the building
of the City. But when their Stage began to be cultivated, immediately a
hundred writers arose, in Poetry, Eloquence, History, and Philosophy,
whose Fame took an equal flight with
that of the *Roman* Eagles, and who,
transmitting their immortal works to
posterity, continue the living glories of
that Republick, and the only solid remains of the *Roman* greatness. As with
the *Roman* Stage the rest of their Arts
were cultivated, and improv'd propor-
tionably;

tionably ; as with that in the Age of *Augustus Cæsar*, about two hundred years from the time of *Livius Andronicus*, they reach'd their utmost height, so with that they declin'd in the Reigns of succeeding Emperors.

For the *French*, 'tis yet scarce a hundred years since *Hardy* first appear'd among them : And *Hardy* was the first who began to reform their Stage, and to recover it from the confusion in which it lay before him. And tho I cannot say, that before that time the *French* had no good writers, yet I may safely affirm, that they had but one, who was generally esteem'd throughout the rest of *Europe :* But to reckon all who have since been excellent in Poetry, Eloquence, History and Philosophy, would certainly make a very long and a very illustrious Roll.

'Tis time to come at last to our selves : It was first in the Reign of King *Henry* the Eighth that the Drama grew into form with us : It was establish'd in the Reign of Queen *Elizabeth*, and flourish'd in that of King *James* the First. And tho I will not presume to affirm, that before the Reign of King

D 4 *Henry*

Henry the Eighth we had no good
Writers, yet I will confidently assert,
that, excepting *Chaucer*, no not in any
sort of Writing whatever, we had not
a first rate Writer But immediately
upon the establishment of the Drama,
three prodigies of Wit appear'd all at
once, as it were so many Suns to amaze
the learned world. The Reader will
immediately comprehend that I speak
of *Spencer*, *Bacon* and *Raleigh* ; three
mighty geniuses, so extraordinary in
their different ways, that not only
England had never seen the like before,
but they almost continue to this very
day, in spight of emulation, in spight
of time, the greatest of our Poets,
Philosophers and Historians.

    From the time of King *James* the
First the Drama flourish'd, and the
Arts were cultivated, till the beginning of our intestine broils, in the
Reign of King *Charles* the First ; when
the Dramatick Muse was banish'd, and
all the Arts degraded. For what other
sort of Poets flourish'd in those days?
who were the inspir'd, the celebrated
men ? Why *Withers*, *Pryn*, *Vickars*,
Fellows whose verses were laborious
                              Libels

Libels upon the Art and themselves.
These were the first-rate Poets, and under them flourish'd a herd of Scribblers
of obscurer infamy: Wretches, who
had not desert enough to merit even
contempt; whose works, like abortions, never beheld the light, stifled in
the dark by their own friends, as so
many scandals upon humane nature, and
lamentable effects of that universal
conspiracy of Fools against Right
Reason. And if any one pretends that
Sir *John Denham*, Sir *William Davenant*,
Mr. *Waller* and Mr. *Cowley* writ many of
their Verses in the time of the late Civil Wars; to him I answer, that what
Mr. *Waller* writ was but very little, and
the other three are notoriously known
to have writ in a Country, where the
Stage and Learning flourish'd. So that
nothing among us that was considerable was produc'd in Poetry in the times
of the late Civil Wars, if you except
but the first part of that admirable Satyr against the Muses mortal foe Hypocrisie, which yet neither did nor durst
appear till the restoration of the
Drama.

We

We have seen what the Poets were
that flourish'd in those dismal times,
let us now see what were the Orators? who were the cry'd up Preachers?
why *Calamy, Case, Hugh Peters, Man-
ton, Sibbs.* But what was produc'd in
the other Sciences, that was worthy of
Posterity? what in Philosophy? what
in History? what in Mathematicks?
what could be expected when only hy-
pocritical fools were encourag'd, whose
abominable canting was christn'd Gift,
and their dulness Grace.

But what sort of persons have flourish'd among us since the restoration of
the Drama? Who have been they who
have signaliz'd themselves in the other
kinds of Poetry? So great is the number of those who have writ politely,
that it is comprehensive of all conditions of men. How many have been
justly Renown'd for Eloquence. So
many extraordinary men have distin-
guish'd themselves by preaching, that
to ennumerate them would be an end-
less thing. I shall content my self with
mentioning the late Archbishop and
the present Bishop of *Rochester,* so illustrious for their different Talents, the
one

One for his extream politeneſs , for his grace and his delicacy, the other for his nervous force, and both for their maſculine purity. Who among us are fam'd for Hiſtory? not only the laſt of thoſe great Prelates, but the preſent Biſhop of *Salisbury*, whoſe Hiſtory of the Reformation is ſo deſervedly celebrated by the learned world, whereever *Engliſh* or *French* is known. What proficients have we in Philoſophy? what in Mathematicks? Let all *Europe* reply, who has read, and reading admir'd them. I ſhall content my ſelf with mentioning two of the living Glories of *England*, Mr *Newton* and Mr *Lock*, the one of which has not his equal in *Europe*, and neither of them has his ſuperiour.

Thus have I ſhown you, how Poetry, Eloquence, Hiſtory, and Philoſophy, have appear'd, advanc'd, declin'd, and vaniſh'd with the Drama, not only in *Greece* and ancient *Italy*, but in modern *France* and *England*. So true it is, what was formerly ſo well ſaid, that all thoſe Arts which reſpect humanity, have a certain alliance, and a mutual dependance, and are defended and ſup-

supported by their common confede-
racy.

Thus while I am pleading in defence
of the Stage, I am defending and sup-
porting Poetry, the best and the noblest
kind of writing. For all other Writers
are are made by Precept, and are
form'd by Art; but a Poet prevails by
the force of Nature, is excited by all
that's powerful in Humanity, and is
sometimes by a Spirit not his own exalted to Divinity.

For if Poetry in other Countries has
flourish'd with the Stage, and been with
that neglected, what must become of
it here in *England* if the Stage is ruin'd;
for foreign Poets have found their
publick and their private Patrons.
They who excell'd in *Greece* were encourag'd by the *Athenian* Stage, nay
and, by all *Greece* assembled at their
Olympian, *Isthmean*, *Nemean*, *Pythian*
Games. *Rome* had its *Scipios*, its *Cæsars*,
and its *Mecenas*. *France* had its mag-
nanimous *Richlieu*, and its greater *Lewis*,
but the protection that Poetry has
found in *England*, has been from the
Stage alone. Some few indeed of our
private men have had Souls that have
been

been large enough, and wanted only power. But of our Princes, how few have had
any taste of Arts; nay, and of them
who had some, have had their Heads
too full, and some their Souls too
narrow.

As then in maintaining the cause of
the Stage, I am defending Poetry in
general; so in defending that I am
pleading for Eloquence, for History
and Philosophy. I am pleading for the
reasonable pleasures of mankind, the
only harmless, the only cheap, the only universal pleasures; the nourish-
ments of Youth, and the delights of
Age, the ornaments of Prosperity, and
the surest Sanctuaries of Adversity; now
insolently attempted by furious zeal too
wretchedly blind to see their beauties,
or discern their innocence. For unless
the Stage be encouraged in *England*,
Poetry cannot subsist; for never was
any man a great Poet, who did not make
it his business as well as pleasure and solely
abandon himself to that. And as Poetry
wou'd be crush'd by the ruines of the
Stage; so Eloquence would be misera-
bly maim'd by them; for which, if
action be confess'd the life of it, the
Thea-

Theatre is certainly the best of Schools; and if action be not the life of it, *Demosthenes* was much mistaken.

In Eloquence I humbly conceive that the Pulpit is something concern'd, and by consequence in the Stage; and need not be asham'd to learn from that place which instructed *Cicero*, and which form'd *Demosthenes*. For I cannot forbear declaring, notwithstanding the extream veneration which I have for the Church of *England*, that if in some of our Pulpits, we had but persons that had half the excellence of *Demosthenes*, that had but half the force of his words, and the resistless strength of his Reasoning, and but half his vehement action, we should see quite another effect of their Sermons. Those divine Orators fulminating with their sacred Thunder, would infix terrible plagues in the souls of sinners, and rouze and awake to a new life even those who are dead in sin.

I now come to answer what is objected from Religion; and that is, that tho it should be granted that some little happiness may be deriv'd from the Stage, yet that there is a much better and

and furer way to be happy : For the
only way to be folidly and laftingly
happy even in this life, is to be truly
Religious, the beft Chriftian being always the happieft man. To which I anfwer, That as the Chriftian Religion
contains the beft, nay, the only means
to bring men to eternal happinefs, fo
for the making men happy ev'n in this
life, it furpaffes all Philofophy ; but
yet I confidently affert, that if the Stage
were arriv'd to that degree of purity,
to which in the fpace of fome little
time it may eafily be brought, the frequenting our Theatres would advance
Religion, and confequently the happinefs of mankind, and fo become a part
of the Chriftian duty, which I fhall de-
monftrate when I come to fpeak of
Religion.

The end of the Firft Part.

T H E

THE
USEFULNESS
OF THE
STAGE.

PART II.

CHAP. I.

That the Stage is useful to Government.

SInce in the firſt part of this Trea-
tiſe, we have plainly demonſtrated
that the Stage is inſtrumental to the
E   hap-

happiness of Mankind, and of *English-men* more particularly; and since it is self-evident, that the happiness of those who are govern'd, is the very end and design of all regular Government, it evidently follows, that the Stage which contributes to the happiness of particular men, is conducive to the good of the State. However, I shall descend to shew more particularly, that the Stage is instrumental to the welfare,

First, Of Government in general.
Secondly, of the *English* Government more particularly.
Thirdly, Especially of the present Government.

First, The Stage is instrumental to the welfare of Government in general; which I shall prove,

1. By Reason : And,
2. By Experience.

And first I shall prove by Reason, that the Stage is instrumental to the welfare of Government, and that whether you consider those who govern,

vern, or secondly, those who are governed.

First, If you consider those who govern.

And here it is self-evident, that no man who governs, can govern amiss, as long as he follows the dictates of common Reason. That requires that all who govern, shou'd consult the interest of those who are govern'd, which is inclusive of their own. And those Rulers have always been upon a wrong foundation, who have had an interest distinct from that of their people. Male-administration has always its source from the passions or vices of those who govern.

The passions which cause it, are for the most part Ambition, or the immoderate love of pleasure. Now as Tragedy checks the first, by shewing the great ones of the Earth humbled, so it corrects the last by firing the mind and raising it to something nobler.

The vices which cause the Male-administration of Governours, are either vices of weakness or of malice, the first of which cause Governours to neglect, and the last, to oppress their people. The vices of weakness are inconsiderateness, and effeminacy, inconstancy, and irresolution.

Now nothing can be a better Remedy than Tragedy for inconsiderateness, which reminds men of their duty, and perpetually instructs them, either by its fable or by its sentences, and shews them the ill and the fatal consequences of irregular administration; and nothing is more capable of raising the Soul, and giving it that greatness, that courage, that force, and that constancy which are the qualifications that make men deserve to command others; which is evident from experience. For they who in all Countries and in all Ages have appear'd most to feel the power of Tragedy, have been the most deserving and the greatest of men. *Æschylus* among the *Athenians* was a great Captain, as well as a Tragick Poet; and *Sophocles* was both an able Statesman and a Victorious General. If we look among the *Romans*, the very greatest among them, were particularly they who appear'd so far touch'd by
the

the Drama, as either to write their Plays themselves, or to build their Theatre. Witness *Scipio*, and *Lelius*, and *Lucullus*, and the Great *Pompey*, and *Mecenas*, and *Julius* and *Augustus Cæsar.*

No man among the *French* has shewn so much capacity or so much greatness of mind as *Richlieu* ; and no man among them has express'd so much passion for the Drama, which was so great, that he writ several Plays himself, with that very hand, which at the same time was laying the Plan of the *French* universal Monarchy

Among us the Drama began to flourish in the Reign of Queen *Elizabeth*, and I have been told, that that great Princess appear'd to be so far charm'd with it, as to translate with her own hand a Tragedy from *Euripides.*

That vice of malice which for the most part causes the male-administration of Governours is cruelty, which nothing is more capable of correcting than Tragedy, which by diving into the hidden Springs of Nature, and making use of all that is powerful in her, in order to the moving compassion, has

been

been always found sufficient to soften
the most obdurate heart.

Numerous examples might be
brought of this, but I shall content
my self with that of *Alexander* the *Thes-
salian* Tyrant, as the story is related
by *Dacier*, in the Preface to his Admirable Comment on the Poetick of *Aristotle*. *This barbarous man, says* Dacier,
causing the Hecuba *of* Euripides *to be
play'd before him, found himself so touch'd
that he went out before the end of the
first Act, seeing it would be a shame for
him to be seen to shed tears for the miseries
of* Hecuba, *or the calamities of* Polyxena,
*for him who every day embrued his hands in
the innocent blood of his Subjects. The
truth of it was, that he had some apprehension, lest he should be so far melted,
that he should be forsaken by that spirit
of Tyranny, which had so long possess'd
him, and should go a private person out of
that Theatre, into the which he had en-
tered a Soveraign. Nay, he had like to
have caus'd the Actor who had mov'd him
thus, to be executed ; but the Criminal
was secured by the very remains of that
compassion, which was his only crime.*

That

That which follows is remarkable, and which *Dacier* cites from an ancient Historian. *A very grave Writer, says Dacier, makes a reflection which is very much to my purpose, and which seems of importance to Government. Speaking of the inhabitants of* Arcadia, *he says, that their humanity, and the sweetness of their tempers, and the respect which they had for the Gods; and in a word, the purity of their manners, and all their virtues proceeded principally from the love which they had for Musick, which by its sweetness corrected those ill impressions, which a raw and unwholesom air, together with the hardship which they endured by their laborious way of life, made on their bodies and on their minds.* And he says on the contrary, *that those of* Cynethus *were carried to all sorts of profligate crimes, because that they, renouncing the wise institutions of their ancestors, had neglected an art which was therefore the more necessary for them, because they inhabited that part of* Arcadia, *which was the coldest, and where the Climate was most unequal.* Indeed, there was no Town in all *Greece*, says *Dacier*, that had given such frequent examples of enormous crimes.

And

And if *Polybius*, says he, speaks this in
the behalf of Musick, and accuses *E-
phorus* for having advanc'd a thing that
was very unworthy of him, in asserting
that Musick was invented on purpose
for the deceiving of Mankind, what
may we not justly affirm of Tragedy,
of which Musick is but a little ornament; and which as far transcends it,
as the reasoning Speech of a man excels
the Brutes inarticulate voice, which
never has any meaning

But now we come in the second place,
to shew that the Stage is useful to Government, with respect to those who
are governed, and that whether you
consider them in relation to those who
govern them, or to one another, or to
the common Enemy.

If you consider them in relation to
those who govern them, you will find
that Tragedy is very proper to check
the motions, that they may at any time
feel to rebellion or disobedience, by
stopping the very sources of them; for
Tragedy naturally checks their Ambition, by shewing them the great ones of
the Earth humbled, by setting before
their Eyes, to make use of Mr *Collier's*
                                words,

words, the uncertainty of human greatneſs, the ſudden turns of State, and the unhappy concluſion of violence and injuſtice. Tragedy too, diverts their apprehenſion of grievances, by the delight which it gives them, diſcovers the deſigns of their factious guides, by opening their eyes, and inſtructing them in their duty by the like examples; and laſtly, it diſpels their unreaſonable jealouſies, for people who are melted or terrified with the ſufferings of the great, which are ſet before their eyes, are rather apt to feel a ſecret pleaſure, from the ſenſe that they have, that they are free from the like calamities, than to torment themſelves with the vain and uncertain apprehenſions of futurity. But the Stage is uſeful to Government in thoſe who are govern'd, if they are conſider'd with relation to one another. For Tragedy diverts them from their unjuſt deſigns, by the pleaſure which it gives them; ſince no man as long as he is eaſie himſelf, is in a humour to diſturb others, and by purging thoſe paſſions, whoſe exceſſes cauſe their injuſtice, by inſtructing them in their

duty

duty by its fable and by its sentences, by raising their minds, and setting them above injustice, by touching them with compassion, and making them good upon a principle of self-love ; and lastly, by terrifying them with setting before their eyes, the unhappy conclusion, to use Mt *Collier*'s words, of violence and injustice.

Thirdly, The Stage is useful to Government, by having an influence over those who are govern'd, in relation to the common enemy. For nothing more raises and exalts their minds, and fires them with a noble emulation, who shall best perform their duty : which brings me to the second Head, the shewing the usefulness of the Stage to Government in general, from

II. Experience, and that of
    1. The *Athenian*.
    2. The *Roman*.
    3. The *French*, and
    4. The *English* Government.

    1. For the *Athenians*, their Drama first appear'd in form with *Thespis*, was cultivated by *Æschylus*, and perfected by *Sophocles*. Now this is extreamly remarkable, that that people, which

which from *Theseus* to *Thespis*, that is, for the space of about seven hundred years, continued a poor and ignorant, and comparatively a contemptible people; in the space of a hundred years more, in which time their Tragedy was form'd by *Thespis*, cultivated by *Æschylus*, and perfected by *Sophocles*; I say, it is extreamly remarkable, that in that space of time, this people, which before were so inconsiderable, became illustrious for Arts and Arms, renown'd for Eloquence, for Philosophy famous, and for Empire formidable, the masters of *Greece*, the scourges of *Asia*, and the Terror of the great King.

In that space of time flourish'd most of their mighty Conquerors, *Cimon*, *Aristides*, *Pericles*, *Themistocles* and *Miltiades*. Their Tragick Poets were the persons who animated their Armies, and fir'd the souls of those brave men, who conquer'd at once and dy'd for their Country, in the Bay of *Salamis*, and in the Plains of *Marathon*; at which place a handful of men, as it were, of the disciples of *Thespis* and the succeeding Poets, vanquish'd the numberless

forces

forces of the East, laid the foundation of the *Grecian* Empire, and of the fortune of the great *Alexander*.

The *Athenians* were highly sensible of the advantage which the State receiv'd from the Theatre, which they maintain'd at a publick prodigious expence, and a Revenue appropriated to that peculiar use ; and establish'd a Law, which made the least attempt to alienate the Fund capital. So that when the common Exchequer was exhausted, *Demosthenes* was oblig'd to use the utmost address to induce them to touch and divert this separate Fund.

But 'tis time to come to the *Romans*. *Livius Andronicus*, who was their first Dramatick Poet, appear'd in the five hundred and fourteenth year after the building of the City. And till his time they had been struggling as it were for life with their neighbours, and had been torn by perpetual convulsions within themselves ; whereas after the first representation of the Plays which were written by him, they were not only quiet within themselves for above a hundred years after, but in a hundred more became the Masters of the Universe.

verſe. And who were the perſons a-
mong them that advanced their Con-
queſts, and extended their Empire?
Why the very men who built their
Theatres and who writ their Plays,
Scipio, conquer'd *Spain* and *Africa*,
Pompey and *Lucullus Aſia*, and *Cæſar
England, Flanders, France*, and *Ger-
many*.

'Tis not above a hundred years ago,
ſince Dramatick Poetry begun to flouriſh in *France*, ſince which time the
French have not only been remarkably
united, but have advanced their Conqueſts ſo faſt, that they have almoſt
doubled their Empire.

Cardinal *Richelieu* was the perſon
who at the ſame time laid the foundation of the greatneſs of their Theatre
and their Empire: And 'tis a ſurprizing
thing to conſider, that the ſpirit of
Dramatick Poetry leaving them juſt
before the beginning of the laſt War,
by *Moliere* and *Corneille*'s Death, and by
Racine's Age, they have ſince that time
loſt almoſt half their Conqueſts.

To come home to our ſelves, Dramatick Poetry began to be brought
into form with us, in the time of *Henry*
the

the Eighth, and tho since that time we cannot boast of such glorious successes, as we had in the times of our Fifth *Henry* and of our Third *Edward*, when the Conquering Genius of *England* in triumph seem'd to bestride the Ocean, and to fix an Imperial foot on the Continent; yet this may be said to the advantage of the Drama, that since it first began to be cultivated, we have had our eyes more open, have found that our constitution is but ill design'd for conquest; that by being very fortunate we should run the risk of becoming very unhappy, and endanger our Liberties, by extending our Empire.

C H A P.

CHAP. II.

That the Stage is particularly useful to the English, *and especially the present Government.*

WE have fhewn in the foregoing Chapter, that the Drama, and particularly Tragedy, is among other reafons ufeful to Government, becaufe it is proper to reftrain a people from rebellion and difobedience, and to keep them in good correfpondence among themfelves : For this reafon the Drama may be faid to be inftrumental in a peculiar manner to the welfare of the *Englifh* Government; becaufe there is no people on the face of the Earth fo prone to rebellion as the *Englifh,* or fo apt to quarrel among themfelves. And this feems very remarkable, that since

since the Drama began first to flourish among us, we have been longer at quiet than ever we were before since the Conquest ; and the only Civil War which has been amongst us since that time, is notoriously known to have been began and carry'd on by those who had an utter aversion to the Stage ; as on the other side, he who now discovers so great an aversion to the Stage, has notoriously done all that lay in his little power to plunge us in another Civil War.

But the Stage is more particularly instrumental to the welfare of our present *English* Government, as the Government is depending upon two things, 1. The Reformation, and 2. The Revolution. I shall speak of the Reformation when I come to treat of Religion. I shall shew at present that the Stage is advantageous to the Government, as it stands since the Revolution ; and that will appear, if we consider what people they are who frequent our Theatres. And they are either friends to the Government, or enemies, or indifferent persons. They who are friends to it, are for the most part so, because

it

it, defends and maintains the liberties of the people. But liberty is a jest if you take away reasonable pleasure; for what would signifie liberty, if it did not make me happier than him who is not free?

Machiavel says, in the 19th Chapter of his *Prince*, that nothing renders a Prince so odious, as the taking possession of the Wives and Estates of his people, that is, nothing renders him so odious as the depriving his Subjects of their lawful and reasonable pleasures; for no mans Wife or Estate is dear to him any further than as they contribute to his pleasure and to his happiness. Now that the Drama is of the number of lawful and reasonable pleasures, has been, and shall be prov'd; and has been all along implied, not by the connivance, but by the authority and the command of so many of our Monarchs, the protection of so many illustrious Princes, and the support and encouragement of so many extraordinary men, who have compos'd for so long together the great Council, of the Nation, whose united judgments ought

F certainly

certainly to be preferr'd before the
pretended opinions of two or three
unknown Bigots, who, under the au-
fterity of their affected grimaces, are
carrying forward their dark defigns,
and could never do a thing upon which
they would esteem themselves more,
than upon depriving the Government
of any of its faithful Friends. And it
is more than probable, that some of
its friends would prove averse to it, if
the Stage were either suppress'd or
very much discourag'd. But in the next
place, the Stage is of use to the Government, if you confider its Enemies ;
for it gives the Enemies of the State a
confiderable diversion. People will
not so furioufly desire a change, as long
as they live agreeably. Men must be
uneasie some way or other in their
manner of living, before they come to
private cabals and plotting. They
who are happy appear averse to them,
and to frequenting Jacobite Conven-
ticles, and to contributing to our non
swearing Parsons. *Hinc illæ Lachrymæ* ;
from hence comes the impotent rage
of our foes, from hence their diffem-
                                    bled

bled zeal; for as long as the enemies of the State are diverted by publick spectacles, their seditious Preachers must be in a wretched condition.

But farther, the Stage is beneficial to the present Government, if you consider a third sort of people who daily frequent it, and they are such who are always indifferent what Government they live under, so they can live but agreeably. Now these are of all others the most addicted to their pleasures, and would take it most heinously to be depriv'd of them.

Thus is the Stage beneficial to the present Government, if you consider those who are friends to it, or enemies, or indifferent. And the same may appear, from considering them all together. For nothing tends to the uniting men more, than the bringing them frequently together, and the pleasing them when they are assembled.

Thus have we shewn, that the Stage is beneficial to the *English* Government, and more particularly to the present Government; and that from the nature of the people, and the conside-

ration

ration of those who frequent our Theatres; we come now to answer what has been, or what may be objected from Reason, from Authority, and from Religion.

C H AP.

CHAP. III.

The Objections from Authority Answer'd.

WE will begin with the objections which are brought from Authority ; the Authorities are numerous which Mr *Collier* has produced in the laſt Chapter of his Book ; which Chapter is levell'd againſt the Stage and Dramatick Poetry in general, as any one may ſee by peruſing the firſt Paragraph. Now I would fain aſk Mr *Collier* one queſtion, whether the buſineſs of Plays is not to recommend Virtue and diſcountenance Vice, and to bring every thing that is ill under infamy and neglect ; whether the Poets, if they pleas'd, might not be ſerviceable to this purpoſe? And the Stage be very ſigniſicant ? What will he ſay to this ? Will he deny it ? Why then did he affirm

F 3   it

it in these very words in his Introduction to his Book? Well, will he confess
it? Then why this pedantick scrowl
of Authorities, to oppose the truth? or
of what significancy is Human Authority against Human Reason? But yet,
to shew the ungenerous temper of this
adversary to Dramatick Poetry, and
consequently to Human Learning, I
shall make it appear, that of all the
Authorities which he has produc'd, several make in defence of the Stage,
and not one of them makes against it.

The objections are of two sorts.
Those opinions of particular Statesmen,
and the sentiments of States in general.
We shall answer the Authorities which
are brought from both, in the same
order as they are cited by Mr. *Collier*.

The two first which he brings are
Plato and *Xenophon*, in the 234th Page.
Plato, says Mr *Collier*, has banish'd
Plays from his Commonwealth: But
what can be concluded from thence?
That they ought to be expell'd from
the *English* Government? When every
Body knows that the Commonwealth
of *Plato* is a meer Romantick notion,
with which human nature, and human
life,

life, and by confequence Dramatick
Poetry, cannot poffibly agree. *Machi-
avil* may give a folid anfwer to this in
the fifteenth Chapter of his *Prince.
Some men,* fays he, *have form d S a es
and Soveraignties in their own fancies,
fuch as never were, and as never will be.
But the diftance is fo very great between
what men are, and between what they ought
to be, that the Statefman who leaves that
which is, to follow that which ought to be,
feeks his own deftruction rather than his
prefervation. And by confequence, he who
makes profeffion of being perfectly good,
among too many others who are not perfectly fo, fooner or later muft certainly
perifh.*

But what has thus exafperated *Plato*
againft the Drama? Why it raifes the
paffions, fays he, and is by confequence
an Enemy to Morality. But *Ariftotle,*
who, as Mr *Collier* in this very page
unhappily owns, faw as far into human
nature as any man; *Ariftotle* has declar'd, that Tragedy, by exciting the
paffions purges them, and reduces them
to a juft mediocrity, and is by confequence a promoter of virtue.

F 4 As

As *Plato* has laid the Plan of a notional Commonwealth, *Xenophon* has given an account in his *Cyropedia* of a Romantick Monarchy; in which he says, that the *Persians* would not suffer their youth to hear any thing that was Amorous or Tawdry. But what can this man mean by bringing this as an authority against the Stage, and the Drama in general: For can any one be so absurd as to imagin, that this was intended by *Xenophon* to condemn the gravity, and severity, and majesty of *Euripides*'s Plays? Those Plays which are said to be in part the productions of the wisest and most virtuous of all the Philosophers, of *Xenophon*'s honour'd incomparable Master, *Socrates*.

The next, whose Authority is produc'd, is *Aristotle*; produc'd? for what? why to overthrow the Authority of that very sort of Writing, which is establish'd upon his own rules. Well! And what says *Aristotle*! Why in his Politicks he lays it down for a rule, that the Law ought to forbid young people the seeing of Comedies Such permissions not being safe, till

age

age and difcipline had form'd them
in fobriety, fortify'd their virtue, and
made it as it were proof againft Debauchery. And what are thefe words
of *Ariftotle* cited to fhew ? Why that
Plays in general are the nurferies of
Vice, the corruption of youth, and
the grievance of the Country,
where they are fuffer'd ; for that was
the thing which in the firft Paragraph
of this fixth Chapter, Mr *Collier* propounded to fhew. Now can any thing
in nature be more unreafonable than
this ?

For in the firft place it can never be,
no, not fo much as pretended, that *A-*
riftotle in this place requires the forbid-
ding any thing but only Comedy,
which is but one fort of Dramatick
Poetry ; nor can it be fo much as pretended, that he requires, that this
fhould be forbidden to any but Boys.
Nor, fecondly, is it probable that *Ari-*
ftotle meant this of any thing but only
that fort of ancient Comedy, which
has no refemblance with ours. For I
have two reafons to perfwade me, that
Ariftotle meant this of only the old
and

and the middle Comedy. The first reason is, that in all likelihood *Aristotle* writ his Politicks while he was Governour to *Alexander,* which was before the establishment of the new Comedy. For *Aristotle* in his Morals commends the reservedness of the new Comedy, which may appear from Mr *Collier's* citation in the 16th page of this very Book. The second reason is, That I can hardly believe that *Aristotle* would have left rules for the writing of Comedy, if he had believ'd that Comedy in general is a Corrupter of Youth. What then *Aristotle* in all probability meant only of the horrible licence of the old and middle Comedy, which yet he requires to be forbidden only to Boys, is here implied to be levelled against Dramatick Poetry in general ; when this very Philosopher has declared, that nothing is more proper than Tragedy for the entertainment even of youth, pronouncing it more grave and more moral than History, and more instructive than Philosophy.

The

The next who enters the Lifts is *Ci-cero*, who, as Mr *Collier* assures us, crys out upon licentious Plays and Poems, as the bane of sobriety and wise thinking, and says, that Comedy sub-fists upon Lewdness. To which I Answer.

First, That *Cicero* in this place speaks only against the corruptions of the Stage, which corruptions we do not pretend to defend.

Secondly, That *Cicero* in his fourth Book of the *Tusculan* Questions, speaks only against Comedy, which is but one sort of Dramatick Poetry, whereas in the very same place he implicitely com-mends Tragedy.

Thirdly, That even in condemning of Comedy he is inconsistent with him-self: And that if the opinion of *Cicero* is of any validity, it is as valuable *pro* as *con*. *Cicero* in his Treatise *De Ami-citia* and *De Senectute*, implicitely com-mends Comedy. For *Lelius*, whom *Cicero* by the mouth of *Fannius*, extols above all the celebrated Seven whom *Greece* renown'd for Wisdom ; *Lelius*, who had the universal reputation of the greatest Statesman, of the best man, and

and the truest friend of his time, : this
Lelius in the Treatise which bears his
name, is not only found to cite a verse
with approbation from *Terence*, but to
mention his acquaintance and intimacy
with that Comick Poet. Now I leave
it to any one to judge, whether *Cicero*
had not been very absurd, if he had
introduc'd a person whom he so much
extols as *Lelius*, a person of that Gravity, and that Capacity, and one who
had so considerable a share in the Government of the *Roman* State : had not
Cicero, I say, been very absurd, if he
had introduc'd a person whom he so
much extols as *Lelius*, openly acknow-
ledging a familiarity with a profest
corrupter of the people? But further,
Cato in that Treatise of *Cicero* which
bears his name, that *Cato* whom *Cicero*
by the mouth of this very *Lelius*, pre-
fers for wisdom to *Socrates* himself, the
awful, the grave, the severe *Cato*, and
the austerest of the *Roman* Censors;
this very *Cato* is introduced in the
fore-mention'd Treatise , making
honourable mention of *Plautus* and
Livius Andronicus.

Livy

Livy and *Valerius Maximus* follow. *Livy,* he fays, *reports the original of Plays. He tells us, they were brought in upon the fcore of Religion, to pacifie the Gods, and remove a Mortality. But then he adds, that the motives are good, when the means are ftark naught : That the Remedy is worfe than the Difeafe, and the Atonement more infectious than the Plague.* In anfwer to which, I defire leave to obferve :

Firft, that *Livy* in this place of the original of Plays, fpeaks neither of Tragedy nor of Comedy, nor of the *Satyri* ; which were the third fpecies of the *Roman* Dramatick Poetry ; but only of the rudenefs of the *Ludi Fefcennini.*

Secondly, That *Livy* commends the innocence of Plays, in the purity of their firft inftitution.

Thirdly, That he attributes by manifeft inference the guilt and corruptions of the *Roman* Stage, to things which can have no relation to our *Englifh* Theatres. Which is apparent from his own words. *Inter aliarum parva principia verum, ludorum quoque prima origo ponenda eft, ut appareret quam ab*

fano

*sano initio res in hanc vix opulentis
Regnis tolerabilem insaniam venerit.* A-
mong the small beginnings of other
things, we are obliged to give some account of the original of Theatrical re-
presentations, that it may appear how
a thing that was innocent in its institu-
tion, grew up to so much licentious
fury, as to render them intolerable
even to the most flourishing States.
From whence it is evident, that *Livy* in
this place condemns the corruption
neither of Comedy nor Tragedy, but
either the licentiousness of *Liberius*
his Farces, or the barbarity of the fights
of the Gladiators, or the lewdness of
the Pantomimes motions, or all of them
put together. For it is manifest to any
one, who has the least tincture of the
Roman Learning, that of the Comedies
and Tragedies which were extant in
Livy's time, those were the purest
which had been writ latest.

Fourthly, I desire leave to observe
here, that the latter half of what
Mr *Collier* has father'd upon *Livy*, viz.
*that the motives were sometimes good,
when the means were stark naught. That
the Remedy in this case was worse than*
     the

the Difeafe ; and the Atonement more in-
fectious than the Plague ; has no manner
of foundation in that Hiftorian. From
all which the Reader may difcover the
uncommon Sincerity and Integrity of
this Cenfurer of the Stage. Indeed ,
without giving my felf all this trouble
for the clearing of the bufinefs, I might
have left it to any one to judge, whe·
ther one of *Livy's* extraordinary fenfe,
who courted Reputation and the favour
of the publick, could have fo little
prudence, or fo little good manners,
as to ufe thofe expreffions which Mr
Collier puts in his mouth of the Drama
itfelf, at the time that it was cherifh'd
by the people, fupported by the Magiftrates, and efteem'd a confiderable
part of their Religious worfhip.

Now it is impoffible that any thing
could fhew lefs judgment than the following citation from *Tacitus*, who
blames *Nero,* fays Mr *Collier,* for hiring
decay'd Gentlemen for the Stage ; for
what does Mr *Collier* conclude from
hence ? That *Tacitus* condemn'd the
diverfions of the Stage ? All that can
be reafonably concluded from it is
this, that *Tacitus* was of opinion that
Nero

Nero debas'd the dignity of the *Roman* Nobility, by enrolling some of their Rank among an order of men, which among the *Romans* was reputed infamous. *Tacitus* was too much a Statesman to say any thing against the Stage, especially in the condition in which we are at present. He approves the conduct of *Augustus* in the first of his Annals, who after he had got possession of the Government, honour'd the *Roman* Theatre with his presence, not only out of his own inclination and complaisance to *Mecenas* ; but because he believ'd that reason of State requir'd, that he should sometimes partake of the pleasures of the people. *Tiberius*, says *Tacitus*, was quite of another humour. However, he had too much policy, and too much good sense, to use his new Subjects severely at first, after they had for so long together liv'd a gentle, voluptuous life. Thus far goes *Tacitus* in the first of his Annals, and Monsieur *Amelot* has made this Remark upon the place : A Prince in the beginning of his Reign ought not to alter any of the establish'd Customs, because the people are very unwilling to part with them. To

To what *Tacitus* says of the *German* Women, that they ow'd their Chaftity to their ignorance of thefe diverfions, this may be anfwer'd, That firft, fuppofing *Tacitus* in the right, that can have no reflection on our modern Theatres. For the *Roman* Ladies may very well have been corrupted by the intolerable lewdnefs of the Pantomimes, which lewdnefs has no relation to us. Secondly, It has been obferv d of *Tacitus*, that he is for referring all things to Politicks, even things that ought to be referr'd to Nature, and is for that reafon fometimes out ; as it is manifeft from experience he is in this cafe. For the *Germans* are now as much us'd to Plays as the *Spaniards* or the *Italians.* And yet their women are much chafter than the women of thofe two Nations. From whence it is evident, that the *German* women owe their Chaftity to the rudenefs of their manners, and to their want of attraction, and to the coldnefs of their conftitution.

In the hurry of my difpatch, I had almoft forgot to return to *Valerius Maximus* ; *Who,* fays Mr *Collier, being contemporary with* Livy, *gives much the*

G *fame*

same account of the rise of Theatres at
Rome. *'Twas Devotion which built them.*
And as for the performances of those
places which Mr Dryden *calls the orna-*
ments, this Author censures as the blemishes
of Peace. And which is more, he affirms,
that they were the occasions of civil di-
stractions, and that the State first blush'd,
and then bled for the entertainment. He
concludes, the consequences of Plays intol-
lerable, and that the Massilienses *did*
well in clearing the Country of them.
Now here in one citation, Mr *Collier*
has made no less than four or five mi-
stakes, whether through malice or ignorance, I must leave the Reader to
judge. For in the first place, *Valerius*
Maximus censures neither Comedies
nor Tragedies as the blemishes of
Peace, and if Mr *Collier* by Theatre
does not mean them, he means
nothing that concerns us. In the next
place he does not affirm, that either they or any of the publick Spectacles were the occasions of civil distractions. In the third place, He does
not affirm that the State either blush'd
or bled for the representation of Plays.
In the fourth place, The refusal of the

Massilienses

Massilienses to admit of Dramatical re-
presentations can never argue any thing,
not only because the consent of Nations
is against that little State, but because
we cannot conclude from their refusal,
that they did not approve of them.

That all this may appear, I am oblig'd
to transcribe what he says. *Proximus
militaribus institutis ad urbana castra, id
est Theatra gradus faciendus est, quoniam
hæc quoque sepenumero animosas acies in-
struxerunt, excogitataque cultus Deorum
& hominum delectationis causa, non sine
aliquo pacis rubore voluptatem & religio-
nem civili sanguine senicorum portentorum
gratia, macularunt.* From military institut-
ons let us proceed to our City Camps, that is
to Theatres. For these too have often shewn
mighty Armies drawn up, and being first design'd for the worship of the Gods, and for the
delights of men, defil'd our Pleasure and our
Religion with the blood of the people.

Where we may take notice of three
things. 1. That *Valerius Maximus* implicitely commends the original institu-
tion of Theatres. 2. That he charges
that which was blameable in them upon
the combats of the Gladiators. Thirdly,
The representation of Plays was so far

from causing civil distractions, that
upon the first representation of the *Ludi
Fescennini*, 390 years after the building
of the City, the Patr'cians and Plebei-
ans were quiet for above eight years,
which was more than they had been for
above a hundred years before. And
after the first representation of Comedies and Tragedies, which was in the
five hundred and fourteenth year of the
City, there was never any civil dissen-
tion, or at least never but once, till
the sedition of *Tiberius Gracchus*, which
was above an hundred years after. Mr
Collier translates *civili sanguine macularunt, caus'd civil distractions*, as if Plays
were the principal cause of the dissentions between the Commons and the Patri-
cians; whereas those dissentions were
natural to the constitution of the *Roman* State, meer necessary consequences
of enlarging their Empire, and by that
means encreasing the number and
force of the Commons, as *Machiavel*
has declared in the sixth Chapter of the
first Book of his discourses.

As for the *Massilians*, they will be
better included under the Authorities which Mr *Collier* has brought
                                    in

in the second place from States.

In examining the Authorities which Mr *Collier* has brought from States, it will be convenient to say a word to the proceeding of the *Maſſilians*, as it is cited from *Valerius Maximus*; who commends them for refuſing to admit of Plays among them. But firſt, the refuſal of this petty ſtate can be of very ſmall ſignificancy againſt the conſent of nations. Secondly, This refuſal is no ſign of their diſeſteem of the Drama, but only of the prudence of their conduct. For expence, and any thing which looks like magnificence, are deſtructive to little States, which can never ſubſiſt without extream frugality

But the Athenians, ſays Mr *Collier,* for which he cites *Plutarch, thought Comedy ſo unreputable a performance, that they made a Law that no Judge of the* Areopagus *ſhould make one.* To which we reply, that this citation of *Plutarch* is abſolutely falſe; and that if it were true, it could not be ſo much as pretended that it concluded againſt any thing but Comedy, which is but one ſpecies of Dramatick Poetry; and

that

that in reality it would be of no force against that.

What *Plutarch* says, is not that the *Athenians* made a Law, that none of the *Areopagi* should make a Comedy; for one might as well suppose that it should be enacted by an *English* Parliament, that none of the twelve Judges should write a Farce. That which *Plutarch* says is this, that the Council of *Areopagus* establish'd a Law, that no man whatever should make any Comedies. From whence it is manifest, that this law was made in the time of the old Comedy, and long before that came to any perfection, For Comedy, as is apparent from *Aristotle*'s treatise of Poetry, was very much discourag'd at first: Indeed at first they were so intolerably scandalous, that they were thought to be prejudicial to the State. And it was a long time before the Magistrates could be prevail'd upon to be at the expence of the Chorus. But after the Magistrates were at the expence of the Chorus, 'tis absurd to imagine that a Law should be preferr'd against the writing that sort of Poem which was represented at the publick expence.   So

So that a Citation which Mr *Collier*
has brought against the Stage in general,
is of no force we fee againſt Tragedy,
nor againſt the new Comedy, no, nor
ſo much as againſt the old one, as it
ſtood in the time of *Eupolis* and *Ariſto-
phanes.* Mr *Collier* brings the words of
his Authors, but leaves us to look for
their Senſe, and yet he would take it
very ill to have that return'd upon him,
which he has ſaid of Mr *Durfey,* that
he is at leaſt in his Citations, *vox &
præterea nihil.*

But he proceeds to the *Lacedæmonians,*
and ſays, that they who were remarkable for the wiſdom of their Laws,
the ſobriety of their manners, and their
breeding of brave men, would not
endure the Stage in any form, nor under any regulation. This citation too
is from *Plutarch,* and juſt of as much
validity againſt the Stage as the other.
For what can Mr *Collier* conclude from
hence, That the *Spartans* diſapprov d
of the Drama? Why then did they
frequent the Theatre while they ſo
journ'd at *Athens*? As it is plain that
they did, both from the *Cato Major* of
Cicero, and from *Valerius Maximus,*

G 4   Chap.

Chap. 5. Lib 4. All that can be concluded, from what *Plutarch* says of the
Lacedæmonians is, that the Drama was
not so agreeable to the nature of the
Spartan Government, it being incom-
patible with rigid poverty, and with
fewness of Subjects, which as *Machiavel*
observes, in the Sixth Chapter of the
first Book of his Discourses, were the two
fundamentals of their constitution.
But then Mr *Collier* may be pleas'd to
observe, that no sort of Poetry flourish'd in that Government, nor History, nor Eloquence, nor written Philosophy. For as we observed above,
the Arts never flourish'd in any Country where the Drama was decay'd or
discouraged, and in those places where
they have flourish'd, as they have risen
they have sunk with the Stage.

But tho the Drama was inconsistent
with the nature of the *Spartan* Government, it is so remarkably agreeable to
ours, that the Stage with us was never
attempted till the late Civil Wars, and
then too by those who had first broke
in upon our constitution, and as it rose
again with the Hierarchy and with the
Monarchy, we have seen it now attempted

tempted a second time, by those, who
by their writings and by their examples, have strenuously endeavour'd to
ruin both Church and State.

The next Authority is brought from
the *Romans.* Tully *informs us*, says Mr
*Collier, that their predeceſſors counted all
Stage-Plays uncreditable and ſcandalous.
Inſomuch that any* Roman *who turn'd
Actor was not only to be degraded, but
likewiſe as it were diſincorporated, and un-
naturaliz'd, by the order of the Cenſors.*

This, Mr *Collier* tells us, that St. *Auſtin* cites from *Tully* in the fourth
Book *De Repub.* ; to which I could eaſily
anſwer, that the ſame St *Auſtin*, as he
is cited by Mr *Collier* in the 274th page
of his Book, having apparently done
Tully wrong in his citation of one of his
Orations which is extant ; the paſſage
which he cites from the fourth Book
De Republica, which is not come down
to us, may be very juſtly ſuſpected.
This, I ſay, I could eaſily anſwer ; and
to convince the Reader that I have
very good grounds for it, I think my
ſelf oblig'd to make it appear, that
St *Auſtin*, as Mr *Collier* has cited him in
the 274th page of his Book has done
Cicero

Cicero a great deal of wrong. The passage is this. *Their own* Tully's *commendation of the Actor* Roscius *is remarkable.* He was so much a Master, *says he,* that none but himself was worthy to tread the Stage; *and on the other hand, so good a man, that he was the most unfit person of the gang to come there.* Now what will the Reader say, when I make it appear that *Tully* never said any such thing? In order to which, I am oblig'd to transcribe the passage. *Roscius Socium fraudavit? Potest hoc homini huic hærere peccatum? Qui medius Fidius (audacter dico) plus Fidei quam artis: plus veritatis quam disciplinæ possidet in se: quem Populus Romanus meliorem virum quam Histrionem esse arbitratur, qui ita dignissimus est scena propter artificium ut dignissimus sit curia propter abstinentiam.* Has Roscius *defrauded his friend? Can he possibly be guilty of this? Who, by Heavens, (I boldly speak it) has more sincerity, than he has Art, more integrity than he has discipline, who, by the judgment of the* Roman *people, is a better Man than he is a Player, the worthiest of all men to tread the Stage, by reason of his excellent action, and*

the

the worthiest to partake of the Magi-
stracy by reason of his singular modera-
tion.

Now I appeal to the Reader, if this
has so much as the least affinity with
Mr *Collier*'s meaning ? I have all this
while done my utmost to keep my
Temper. But I cannot forbear inform-
ing Mr *Collier*, that Nature did not
make the ferment and rising of the
Blood for Atheism, as he fondly imagins
in the 80th page of his Book. For an
Atheist is a wretched unthinking Creature, who deserves compassion. No,
Nature made the Ferment of the blood
to rise against those, who are base
enough to defame the dead by suborn-
ing them to witness what they never
knew nor thought.

From all which it plainly appears,
that I may deny very justly to answer
to what is cited here from *Cicero*, since
part of it carries in itself such a Mani-
festation of falsehood ; for how could
Plays be accounted scandalous by the
predecessors of *Cicero*, when before the
end of the first *Punick* War, which
was about two hundred years before
Cicero's time, the *Romans* knew nothing

of the true Drama ; for the Plays which were repreſented in the 391ſt year of the City, were the *Ludi Feſcennini*. Now it was not quite a hundred years after the appearance of *Livius Andronicus*, who writ the firſt Plays, that *Scipio* and *Lelius*, the two greateſt men of the State, whether you conſider their virtue, their courage, or their capacity, encourag'd and aſſiſted *Terence* in the writing of his Comedies, and were his friends by publick profeſſion, which they would certainly never have been, if at that time the *Romans* had lookt upon Plays as ſcandalous. 'Tis indeed very true, that the profeſſion of Actor was not very creditable at *Rome*, but it does not follow from thence, that Plays were at all ſcandalous. Your common Fidlers are ſcandalous here, though Muſick is very honourable. The ancient *Romans* could not eſteem any thing that was Religious ſcandalous. Their Plays were a part of their Religious worſhip, repreſented at the publick expence, and by the care of the *Ædiles Curules*, the Magiſtrate; who had the care of the publick worſhip.

I

I muſt confeſs I have a hundred times wondered, why Players that were ſo much eſteem'd at *Athens,* ſhould have ſo little credit at *Rome,* when the Plays had ſo much, when not only both Tragedies and Comedies were a part of their Religious worſhip, repreſented at the expence of the publick, and by the care of the publick Magiſtrates, but when the very perſons who writ 'em were careſt by their greateſt Stateſmen, nay, and when ſome of the Poems were written by their greateſt Stateſmen themſelves.

But *Livy,* whom Mr *Collier* cites once again, ſhall immediately clear my doubt, for the young *Romans,* ſays he, according to Mr *Collier*'s citation, kept the *Fabulæ Atellanæ* to themſelves. They would not ſuffer this diverſion to be blemiſh'd by the Stage. For this reaſon, ſays Mr *Collier,* as the Hiſtorian obſerves, the Actors of the *Fabulæ Atellanæ,* were neither expell'd their Tribe, nor refus'd to ſerve in Arms. Both which penalties it appears the common Players lay under.

Here

Here Mr *Collier* seems to me, to have
made a very gross mistake. For he has
interpreted *ab Histrionibus Pollui to
be blemish'd by the Stage*, according to
the noble Latitude which he gives
himself in translating. Whereas it is
very plain from *Horace*'s Art of Poetry,
that the *Fabulæ Atellanæ* were acted
on the publick Theatre immediately
after the Tragedies.

*Verum ita Risores, ita Commendere
                                                dicaces
Conveniet Satyros, ita vertere seria
                                                ludo;
Ne quicunq; Deus, quicunque adhibe-
                                                bitur Heros
Regali conspectus in Auro nuper &
                                                ostro,
Migret in obscuras humili Sermone Ta-
                                                bernas.*

Dacier is of opinion too in his Comment
on the 227th verse of *Horace*'s Art of Poetry, that the *Fabulæ Atellanæ* were not
only acted on the publick Stage, but acted
by the same Players that the Tragedies
were, in which he is apparently mistaken;
for in the first place this opinion makes
                                                him

him inconsistent with himself; as any one may see, who consults what he says, upon the 231st verse, where he affirms, that the Actors of the *Fabulæ Atellanæ*, had priviledges beyond what the common Players had. In the second place, the passage which he brings to prove his opinion, proves nothing at all. The Passage is,

Regali conspectus in auro nuper & ostro, *&c.* which *Dacier* takes to be spoken of the Players, whereas it is manifestly spoken of the *Persona Drammatis,* that is, of the God or the Heroe.

From what I have said, we may observe three things.

First, That the *Fabulæ Atellanæ* were acted on the publick Theatre. Secondly, That they were not acted by the Tragedeans nor the Comedians, tho they were writ by the Tragick and Comick Poets. Thirdly, That the Actors of the *Fabulæ Atellanæ* were not better treated than common Actors, because they did not Act on the publick Theatre. *Valerius Maximus* gives us the reason why they were better treated in the Fourth Chapter of his Second Book.

Book. *Atellani autem ab oscis acciti*
sunt: quod genus detectationis Italica se-
veritate temperatum ideoq; vacuum notâ
est, nam neque tribu movetur, neque a
militaribus stipendiis repellitur. From
whence it is apparent, that it was from
the severity of that sort of Pöem, that
the Actors of the *Fabulæ Atellanæ* were
treated more kindly, than the common
Actors.

But now how came the Actors of
the *Fabulæ Atellanæ* to be treated with
so much humanity, on the account of
the severity of those Poems, when the
Tragedians incurr'd the Censorian
note ? For Tragedy has infinitely more
severity than the *Fabulæ Atellanæ* could
ever have. For the *Fabulæ Atellanæ*
were partly satyrical, and had as great
a mixture of Raillery as have our
Tragi Comedies ; whereas Tragedy as
all the world knows is grave and severe throughout. That which follows
seems to me to be the reason of this,
and to be the true cause why at *Rome*
the common Actors were so hardly us'd,
when Plays were so much esteem'd by
the *Romans.*

The

The first Plays that were reprefented by the *Romans* were the *Ludi Fefcennini*, which were licencious and fcurrilous even at firft, and full of particular fcandalous reflections, but in a little time they grew bloody and barbarous; 'and that cruelty of Defamation to which they arriv'd, was in all probability the caufe why thofe who acted in them were fo feverely treated by the State. And what inclines me to this opinion the more, is the following paffage of *Horace*.

Fefcennina per hunc inventa Licentia
                   morem,
Verfibus alternis approbria ruftica fudit,
Libertafque recurrentes accepta per an-
                   nos
Lufit Amabiliter : donec jam fervus
                   apertam
In Rabiem verti cæpit Jocus; & per
                   honeftas
Ire domos impune minax : Doluere
                   cruento
Dente lacessiti : fuit intactis quoꝗ cura
Conditione fuper communi : Quis etiam
                   Lex
Pænaꝗ lata.

H   Not

Not long after these appear'd the *Fa-bulæ Atellanæ* ; and because their Satyr was free from particular reflection, and their raillery innocent, and because there was something which was severe and noble in them ; this might prevail upon the following censors to exempt the Actors of the *Fabulæ Atellanæ* from the censorian note; and might occasion a Law to be made, that these Actors should be capable of bearing Arms.

It was a considerable time after this before Tragedies and Comedies were substituted in the room of the *Ludi Fescennini*. Comedy at first was cultivated most, as *Dacier* somewhere observes, and it was late before Tragedy arriv'd to its height, tho at the last it fell infinitely short of the divine sublimity of the *Sophoclean* Tragedy. Now tho the *Romans* were charm'd with Tragedy when it was come to its height, and consequently with those who writ it, and tho they found it to be without comparison more grave, more noble, and more instructive than the *Fabulæ Atellanæ* were, yet they might probably think it below the majesty of the *Roman* people to abolish an ancient custom, and

and an eftablifh'd Law of the State, in
favour of the common Players. Yet
this can be of no prejudice to our modern Players ; becaufe all States have
had unreafonable cuftoms, and this of the
Romans may be concluded to be fuch ;
being directly oppofite to that of the
Grecians, and the *Athenians* particularly, from whom the *Romans* had their
Laws of the twelve Tables, which were
the moft venerable of all their Laws.
What I have already faid anfwers the
Theodofian Code , and fo I come to that
which he calls our own conftitution;
from that which breaks our conftitution.

Neither of the two Statutes, which
he mentions page 242, can reach the
King and the Queens Servants, they
being by no means in the rank of common Players. The Theatre flourifh'd
under the Princes in whofe Reigns thofe
Statutes were made, efpecially in the
Reign of the latter, which may ferve
for a proof that the feverity of
that Statute extended only to Strowlers.

All that can be concluded from the
Petition to Queen *Elizabeth,* which is
mentioned in the fame page, is that

H 2   the

the Queen thought fit to suppress the
Play-houses that were set up in the City,
tho she allow'd them in other places.
And this was not without a great deal
of Reason : For since the Interest of
England is supported by Trade, and
the chief Trade of *England* is carry'd on
by the Citizens of *London*, it was not
convenient that the young Citizens
should have a temptation so near them,
that might be an avocation to them
from their affairs. And since it is apparent from Mr *Collier's* citation, that
the Queen, upon the City's Remon-
strance, supprest the Play-houses which
were set up in the City, but suffer'd
them in other places; this very citation
is a manifest proof of that Queens approbation of Theatres and Dramatick
Poems.

  That Reader who can expect that I
should make any serious answer to the
following citations from the Bishop of *Ar-*
ras's decree and the *Dutch* Gazette, deserves to be laught at rather than satisfy'd.
And I cannot imagine why these Ga-
zettes should be cited in the same row
with so many Philosophers, **Councils**
and

and Fathers, unless Mr *Collier* would
slily insinuate that they are of equal
Authority. But 'tis high time to proceed to the objections which may be
brought from Reason and Religion.

H 3 CHAP

C H A P. IV.

The Objections from Reason and Religion Answer'd.

I Now come to answer what may be
objected from Reason and from
Religion.

The objections against the Stage,
from Reason are chiefly four. 1. That
it encourages Pride. 2. That it encourages Revenge. 3. That it exposes
Quality; and by doing so, brings a
considerable part of the Government
into Contempt.

4. That it exposes the Clergy, and
by endangering Religion endangers
Government. The two first are general, and the two last particular objections. I shall speak to them all suc-
cinctly.

First, The Stage encourages Pride;
a quality that indisposes men for obe-
dience,

dience, and for the living peaceably. To which I anſwer, that if Ambition is meant by Pride, the Stage is ſo far from encouraging that, that it is the buſineſs of Tragedy to deter men from it, by ſhewing the great ones of the Earth humbled. On the other ſide, if Pride be made to ſignifie Vanity, and Affectation, the child of Vanity, 'tis the buſineſs of Comedy to expoſe thoſe; which is ſufficiently acknowledg'd by Mr *Collier* in the Introduction to his Book. But if by Pride is meant Pride well regulated, which Philoſophers call Greatneſs of mind, and which men of the world call Honour, then I muſt confeſs that the Stage above all things encourages that, and by encouraging it provides for the happineſs of particular men, and for the publick proſperity.

I muſt confeſs, if all men were perfect Chriſtians, there would be no occaſion for this Philoſophical Virtue. But ſince that neither is, nor, if we credit the Scriptures, will be, and ſince this very Pride is the Virtue of thoſe who are not Virtuous, and the Religion of thoſe who are not Religious, I

ap-

appeal to any sensible Reader, if it is not to this that he owes in some measure his life, his fortune, and all his happiness. For it is this, which in a great measure makes his Servant just to him, his Friend faithful, and his Wife chaste.

'Tis this too from whence for the most part comes the security and ornament of States. The love of Glory goads on the conquering Souldier to his duty, excites the Philosopher, animates the Historian, and inflames the Poet. So that, in short, from this very quality, the encouraging which Mr *Collier*'s undistinguishing Pen condemns, proceed almost all the advantages that make private men happy, and States prosperous.

But Secondly, The Stage encourages Revenge, which is so destructive to the happiness of particular men, and to the publick Peace. To which I answer, First, that the Stage keeps a man from revenging little injuries, by raising his mind above them. Secondly, That if it does sometimes show its Characters revenging intolerable injuries, and consequently punishing enormous crimes,

yet

yet by doing that it deters men from committing such crimes, and consequently from giving the occasions of such Revenge: So that we may set the one against the other. Thirdly, That perhaps it equally concerns the peace of mankind, that men should decline the revenging little injuries which happen every day, and should sometimes revenge intolerable ones, which very seldom happen. *Cicero* affirms in his Oration for *Milo*, that *Milo* had done a service to the Commonwealth by removing of *Cloudius*. From whence it appears, that that great Statesman thought that sometimes private Revenges might be necessary for the publick Safety. *Servilius Ahala* did service to the State by removing of *Spurius Melius*; and *Scipio Nasica* sav'd it from utter ruin by the Death of *Tiberius Gracchus*. Fourthly, That sort of Tragedy, in which the Characters are the best form'd, and the incidents the best contriv'd to move Compassion and Terror, has either no Revenge, or by no means that sort of Revenge which can encourage the Crime in others. If Mr *Collier* had known any thing of a Play,

Play, he would have been sensible of
this. If any Reader wants to be convinc'd of it, I refer him to what I have
cited from *Aristotle*'s Poetick in the last
Chapter of the Remarks on *Prince Arthur*. But,

Thirdly, The Stage exposes the Nobility, and so brings a part of the Government into contempt. This objection
seems to Mr *Collier*, peculiar to the
English Stage. For as for *Moliere*, says he,
he pretends to fly his Satyr no higher
than a Marquis. Good God! As if a
Marquis were not above any condition
of men that have been expos'd on the
English Stage. This trick that our
Poets have got of exposing quality, is
a liberty, says Mr *Collier*, unpractis'd
by the *Latin* Comedians : where, by
Comedians, I suppose, he means Comick
Poets. But it was very common with
the *Greeks*, *Aristophanes*, *Cratinus*, *Eupolis*, and all Writers of the old Comedy, not only expos'd the chief of
the *Athenian* Nobility, but mention'd
their very names, and produc'd their
very persons by the resemblance of
the Vizors. In imitation of these, *Lu-
cilius* the Inventor of Satyr, as *Horace*
                                                  tells

tells us, spar'd none of the *Roman* Nobility, if they deserv'd the lash, no, not even persons of Consular dignity. And yet as *Boileau* observes in his discourse upon Satyr, *Scipio*, and *Lelius*, did not think this man unworthy of their friendship, because he had expos'd some of the scandals to quality, and did not imagin that they in the least endanger'd their own Reputation, by abandoning all the Coxcombs of the Commonwealth to him. From whence 'tis apparent, that if the *Roman* Comick Poets did not bring the Nobility of *Rome* upon the Stage, it was for want of opportunity and not of good will. For how should they bring the *Roman* quality upon the Stage, when it is plain that they never laid their Scene in *Rome*, nor so much as in *Italy*. The *Latin* Comick Poets translated the *Greeks*; now the old and the middle Comedy they could not translate, because the old Comedy describing particular persons, and the middle one particular adventures, those Comedies must have lost most of their graces upon the Theatre of another State. The *Latins* then translated the new Comedy, in which

which indeed the *Athenian* Nobility
was never expos'd, because it was im-
practicable in that way of writing.
For the *Athenians* had no Titles among
them ; because those people who were
truly great knew that real greatness
consisted in merit and virtue ; but when
that real greatness forsook the world,
a titular greatness, the shadow of the
other, was introduced to supply it ; a
meer invention to cajole people, and
perswade them that they might be
noble without Virtue. Now the *Athe-*
nians having no Titles, I cannot conceive how the *Athenian* Nobility could
be possibly expos'd by *Menander*, or
any of the Writers of the new Comedy.
For, to set the mark of Quality on any
one of their Characters, there was either
a necessity of mentioning his name, or
describing his person, or his particular
employment in the State ; the doing
which would have thrown them back
upon the old or middle Comedy, which
were both forbid by the Law. From
all which it appears, that the *Romans*
in this case are not against us, and the
French are clearly on our sides. But to
come to the reason of the thing, if a
                                          Lord

Lord may not be shewn a Fool upon the Stage, I would fain ask Mr *Collier* what Fools a Comick Poet may lawfully show there, and at what condition of men he is oblig'd to stop. I would fain know whether a Poet may be allow'd to Dub his Dramatical Coxcombs? May he show a Fool a Knight Baronet, or a Knight Batchelour, or are they too included in Quality? Must he be oblig'd to go no further than Squire, and must Fool and Squire continue to be terms synonimous? If any of Mr *Collier*'s acquaintance will give himself the diversion of asking him these questions, I dare engage that he will find him embarass'd sufficiently.

But methinks neither the Lords nor we are oblig'd to Mr *Collier* for his extraordinary civility. For if a Lord is capable of committing extravagancies as well as another man, why should Mr *Collier* endeavour to perswade him that he is above it? or why should he hinder him from being reclaim'd? unless he would imply that a Commoner may be corrected when he grows extravagant, but that when a Lord grows fantastick he is altogether incorrigible. Nor are

we

we oblig'd to Mr *Collier* any more than the Peers are? For since the bare advantage of their conditions makes some of them already grow almost insupportable, why should any one endeavour to add to their vanity, by exempting them from common censure?

Besides, since follies ought to be expos'd, the follies of the great are the fittest, as being most conspicuous and most contageous. The follies of the meaner sort are often the effects of ignorance, and merit compassion rather than contempt. Affected follies are the most despicable; now Affectation is the child of Vanity, and Vanity of Condition.

But why should a Lord be free from Dramatical censure, when he can be corrected no where but upon the Stage? A Commoner may be corrected in company, but such friendly admonition to a Lord may be interpreted Scandal.

For our Comick Poets, I dare engage that no men respect our Nobility more than they do: They know very well that their titles illustrate their merit, and adorn their virtue; but that those whom they expose, are such
whose

whofe Follies and whofe Vices render their Titles ridiculous. And yet that they expofe them no more than the reft of the Kings Subjects : For Folly as well as Vice is perfonal, and the Satyr of Comedy falls not upon the order of men, out of which the Ridiculous Characters are taken, but upon the perfons of all orders who are affected with the like follies.

For they know further what Mr *Collier* apparently never knew, that a Lord in effect in a Comedy fignifies any man: For the Characters of Comedy are always at bottom univerfal and allegorical: And the making Lords of their Comick Fools, can fignifie no more than to admonifh our men of Quality that they are concern'd in the inftruction as well as others.

The fourth objection from Reafon is, That the Stage expofes the Clergy, and fo by endangering Religion endangers Government. But of this I fhall fpeak in the following part of this Book, where I defign to treat of Religion.

We now come to anfwer what is objected from Religion, which is, That there is no need of the Stage to make
people

people good Subjects; for that the Pulpit teaches men their duty to their Prince, better than all the Philosophy and all the Poetry in the world. 'Tis indeed undeniable. But the validity of this objection depends upon two suppositions; which are, that all the Subjects of the State go to Church, and that all attend when they are there. Whereas it is manifest that our Atheists and Deists seldom go thither; and that our doubting, cold, and lukewarm Christians seldom attend when they are there. But that the Stage, reduc'd to its primitive purity, would be a means to send them thither, and the best of all human preparatives for the Divine instruction which they would find there, is designed to be shown in the remaining part of this Treatise.

The end of the second part.

THE

THE
USEFULNESS
OF THE
STAGE.

PART III.

CHAP. I.

That the Stage is useful to the Advancement of Religion.

I Now come to shew that the Stage is useful to the advancement of Religion.

I

ligion. And, First, Of the Christian
Religion in general. Secondly, Of the
Christian Religion particularly, and
more especially of the Reform'd Religion.

Religion in general, or natural Religion, may be consider'd as consisting of
two parts; the things to be believed,
and the things to be done.

First, The things to be believed, are
1. The being of a God. 2. Providence.
3. Immortality of the Soul. 4. Future
Rewards and Punishments. The Poet,
and particularly the Tragick Poet, af-
serts all these, and these are the very
foundations of his Art; for in the first
place the Machines are the very life
and soul of Poetry; now the Machines
would be absurd and ridiculous without the belief of a God, and a particular Providence. In the second place,
let any man shew me where Terror is
mov'd to a heighth, and I will shew
him that that place requires the belief
of a God and particular Providence.
In the third place, Poetick Justice would
be a jest if it were not an Image of the
Divine, and if it did not consequently
suppose the being of a God and Providence.

dence. It ſuppoſes too the immortality of the Soul, and future rewards and puniſhments. For the things which in perfect Tragedy bring men into fatal calamities are involuntary faults; that is, faults occaſion'd by great paſſions. Now this upon a ſuppoſition of a future ſtate, is very juſt and reaſonable. For ſince paſſions in their exceſſes, are the cauſes of moſt of the diſturbances that happen in the world, upon a ſuppoſition of a future ſtate, nothing can be more juſt, than that the power which governs the world, ſhould make ſometimes very ſevere examples of thoſe who indulge their paſſions; providence ſeems to require this. But then to make involuntary faults capital, and to puniſh them with the laſt puniſhment, would not be ſo conſiſtent with the goodneſs of God, unleſs there were a compenſation hereafter. For ſuch a puniſhment would not only be too rigorous, but cruel and extravagant.

The ſecond part of natural Religion contains the things which are to be done; which include,

1. Our

1. Our duty to God.
2. Our duty to our Neighbour.
3. Our duty to our selves.

And all these it is the business of Tragedy to teach; witness the practice of the Ancient Chorus, as it is comprehended in the following verses of *Horace.*

Ille bonis favet ;, & concilietur Amicis
Et regat irato , & amet peccare timentes :
Ille Dapes laudet mensæ brevis ille
salubrem
Justitiam, legesq; & apertis otia portis :
Ille tegat commissa Deosq; precetur &
oret
Ut redeat miseris, abeat fortuna su-
perbis.

From which it appears, that it was the business of Tragedy to exhort men to Piety and the worship of the Gods; to perswade them to Justice, to Humility, and to Fidelity, and to incline them to moderation and temperance. And 'tis for the omission of one of these duties that the persons of the modern Tragedy are shewn unfortunate in their Catastrophes.   Thus

Thus *Don John* is deſtroy'd for his libertiniſm and his impiety ; *Timon* for his profuſion and his intemperance ; *Macbeth* for his lawleſs ambition and cruelty ; *Caſtalio* for his falſhood to his Brother and Friend ; *Jaffeir* for his clandeſtine Marriage with the Daughter of his Benefactor ; and *Belvidera* for her diſobedience.

Thus we have ſhewn, by reaſon and by matter of fact, that it is the buſineſs of the Stage to advance Religion, and it is plain from Hiſtory and from Experience, that Religion ha flouriſh'd with the Stage ; and that the *Athenians* and *Romans* who moſt encourag'd it, were the moſt religious people in the world. And, perhaps, if we would come down to our ſelves, it would be no difficult matter to ſhew, that they who frequent our Theatres, have a great deal more of natural Religion in them, than its declared inveterate Enemies, who are principally Fanaticks and Jeſuits : for the Vices which are charg'd upon the friends of the Stage, are for the moſt part the effects of frailty, and meer human Vices ; whereas the faults of its inveterate Enemies, are known to be

diabolical

diabolical crimes, destructive of Society, of Peace, and of human Happiness; such as falshood, slander, injustice, back-biting, perfidiousness, and irreconcileable hatred.

I now come to shew in the second place that the Stage is useful for the advancing the Christian, and particularly the Reformed Religion. The Christian Religion has two parts, the Moral and the Mysterious. The Moral consists of Human and Christian Virtues: The Human Virtues are a part of Natural Religion, which, since the Stage advances, as we have shewn above, it follows that it partly advances Christianity. The Stage too in some measure may be made to recommend Humility, Patience and Meekness to us, which are true Christian Virtues: And tho a Dramatick Poet neither can nor ought to teach the Mysteries of the Christian Religion, yet by recommending the Human and the Christian Virtues to the practice of our Audience, he admirably prepares men for the belief of the Mysteries. For this is undeniable, that it is not Reason, but Passion and Vice that keeps any man from being a Christian.

That

That therefore that moderates our Paſſions, and inſtructs us in our Duty, muſt conſequently advance our Faith. So that the Stage is not only abſolutely neceſſary for the inſtructing and humanizing thoſe who are not Chriſtians, but the beſt of all human things to prepare them for the ſublimer Doctrines of the Church. Now that which inclines us to the Chriſtian Religion will incline us to the purer ſort of it, and that which has the leaſt affinity with Idolatry, which is the Reform'd Religion. That which opens men's eyes as the Stage does, by purging our paſſions and inſtructing us in our duty; and that which raiſes their minds, will make them naturally averſe from ſuperſtitious foppery, and from being ſlaves to Prieſtcraft, And that which expoſes Hypocriſy, as the Stage does, muſt naturally make men averſe from Fanaticiſm and the affected auſterity of Bigots. And therefore the Jeſuits on one hand, and the Fanaticks on the other, have always been inveterate Enemies to Plays. This is remarkable, that the Church and the Hierarchy, ever ſince the Reformation, have flouriſh'd with the Stage, were depos'd with it, and

re-

restor'd with it.　Thus have I shewn
that the Stage advances Religion , and
more particularly the Christian Reform'd
Religion.　come now to answer what
may be objected from Reason and from
Authority.

CHAP. II.

The Objections from Reason Answer'd.

THe objections from Reason are
chiefly three. That the Stage makes
its Characters sometimes talk prophanely; that it encourages Pride, that it
exposes Religion in the Priesthood.
These are so easily answer'd, that I
shall dispatch them in a few words, and
come to the objections from Authority.

First, The Stage sometimes makes its
Characters talk prophanely.　To which
I answer;　That if the Character which
speaks is well mark'd and the prophaneness be necessary for the Fable and for
the

the Action, then the prophaneſs is not unjuſtifiable : for to aſſert the contrary, would be to affirm, that is is unlawful for a Dramatick Poet to write againſt prophaneneſs, which is ridiculous. A Poet has no other way in the Drama of giving an Audience an averſion for any Vice, than by expoſing or puniſhing it in the perſons of the Drama. And here I think my ſelf obliged to reply to ſomething that Mr *Coller* has aſſerted, in his Remarks upon Mr *Dryden's King Arthur,* which is, that they who bring Devils on the Stage, can hardly believe them any whereelſe. But why for Godſake ? for a man of ſenſe always reaſons, but the Pedant aſſerts dogmatically. Did *Æſchilus* in bringing the Furies upon the Stage of *Athens,* ſhew that he thought they were nothing but a poetical ſham ? Why ſhould it be more irreligon in us to bring Devils on the Stage, that it was to bring Furies in him ? Can any thing be more terrible, than the ſhewing of Devils, if they are ſhewn ſolemnly ? And can any thing that moves Terror, do a diſſervice to Religion ?

But,

But, Secondly, The Stage encourages Pride. Indeed, I must confess, that even the best sort of Pride, which some call honour, and others greatness of mind, is not so very consistent with some of the Christian virtues. But then I do not affirm that the Stage can be at all useful for the instruction of those who are arrived at any more perfect state of Religion ; but for those who are not, that is, for the generality of Mankind, greatness of mind may be very serviceable, for the assisting them to command their passions, and the restraining them from committing enormous crimes.

But, Thirdly, The Stage exposes Religion by exposing the Priesthood. To which I answer, That to talk of exposing Religion is Cant ; for to expose Religion is to expose Truth, which is absurd ; because nothing can be expos'd but that which is false. If the Stage really ridicul'd Religion, instead of ridiculing Hypocrisie, some people, whose Religion lies in their Muscles, would be more easily reconciled to it. For how many Books have been printed in *English* that have been levell'd directly against Religion itself? For what
                                                     reason

reason then have none of those Zealots, who have declaim'd with so much fury against the Stage, writ any thing to dissuade people from reading those Deistical and Atheistical Treatises? For what reason have they omitted this, unless because those Books only attack Religion, about which they never much trouble their heads: but the Poets attack them. The bringing a vicious or a ridiculous Priest upon the Stage then cannot be interpreted the exposing Religion, but the ridiculing Hypocrisie. However, this is very certain, that no Poet ought to shew a Priest in such a manner as to shew any disesteem of the Character. But I cannot for my life conceive why the bringing a foolish or a vicious Priest upon the Stage should be such an abominable thing.

For, since persons of all degrees, from Monarch to Peasant, are daily brought upon the Stage, why should the Clergy be exempted? The Clergy have been treated by our Comick Poets with a great deal more respect than the Laity : Because they have hardly spar'd any condition of the Laity, but none of the superiour Clergy have been ever ex-

expos'd in our Comedies ; which is one
sign of the good intention of the Poets,
and that they only show the Follies and
Vices of some, while they reverence
the Piety and Learning of others, and
the order in general.

And whereas Mr *Collier* affirms, that
foreign States suffer no Priests to be expos'd on the Comick Stage. To that
we answer, That in Countries where the
Church of *Rome* is establish'd they have
some reason to use this niceness : For
prudence requires that the Magistrate
should always take care of the established Religion, and the established Religion in those Countries being almost all
Priestcraft, to expose the Priests is there
to expose Religion. Besides, in those
places Priestcraft and Secular Policy
have a nearer alliance, and a closer dependance on each other by much, than
they have here : for the Priests are con-
siderably assistant to the Magistrates in
the enslaving the people, Besides, in
Italy and *Spain* the Inquisition rages,
and Priests will be sure to take care of
themselves. As for *France*, tho they
never had a Priest upon the Stage, yet
they have a Poem which was writ on
pur-

pofe to ridicule even the fuperiour Clergy. And by whom was it writ? By Monfieur *Boileau*, the moft fober and moft religious of all their Poets. Who advis'd it? Who commanded it? Monfieur *De Lamoignon*, illuftrious for his profound Capacity, renown'd for his Learning, and fam'd for his Piety; who believ'd that the expofing that litigious humour that was crept into the Regular Clergy, might do important fervice to the *Gallican* Church. And why fhould our Magiftrates make any exception againft the expofing the faults of the Clergy here, where the Religion is fo pure, that to touch a Prieft is by no means to hurt the Religion.

And whereas Mr *Collier* fays, that to affront a Prieft is to affront the Deity; fo it is to a affront a Peafant who is a good Chriftian; befides, affronts are always perfonal, but a Prieft in a Play is a general Character; and the bringing an ill or a ridiculous one upon the Stage, rather proceeds from our veneration for Religion, than from any contempt of it.

And whereas Mr *Collier* takes a great deal of pains to prove that a Prieft ought

ought not to be contemn'd because he
is a degree above a Gentleman ; that
defence methinks is not altogether so
pertinent. For it is evident, that persons of degrees superiour to Gentlemen
are every day expos'd on the Stage.
And besides, the way for a Clergyman
to secure himself from contempt, is not
to boast of secular advantages which in
him is truly ridiculous, but to shew his
Meekness and his Humility, which are
true Christian virtues.

Besides, the Characters in every Comedy are always at the bottom universal and allegorical, or else the instruction could not be universal. A ridiculous or vicious Priest in a Comedy, sig-
nifies any man who has such follies or
vices, and the Cassock is produc'd on
purpose to signify to the Clergy, that
they are partly concern'd in the instruction, and have sometimes their
vices and foilies as well as the Laity.

The exposing upon the Stage a Priest,
who is an ill, or a ridiculous person,
can never make the order contemptible, for nothing can make the Priesthood contemptible but Priests. He
among them who writ the *Grounds of*
the

the Contempt of the Clergy, says nothing
that I remember of the Stage ; but he
says a great deal of their own follies,
and something too of their vices ; now
the exposing these follies and vices,
would be a way to reclaim them, and
so to preserve the esteem that they
have in the world.

This is plain from experience : For
the Inferiour Clergy is much more re-
spected in *England*, than the Regular
Clergy is either in *France* or *Italy*,
where they are never expos'd on the
Stage. And their lives are here less
scandalous than they are abroad. They
who have been at *Marseilles*, may inform
Mr *Collier*, that it is there a very common thing to see Priests, both Secular
and Regular, who are slaves in the Gal-
leys for the most detestable crimes.

It appears to be full as necessary, to
expose a Priest, who is an ill man, as
one of the Laity, because his example
is more contageous, and the salvation
of so many Souls depend on it : whereas
a Layman influences fewer. Besides, a
Layman often offends thro want of
consideration, because he does not reflect, his worldly avocations diverting
his

his thoughts from Religion ; so that
such a one may have returns of Con-
science. But an ill Clergyman cannot
pretend inconsiderateness, for it is his
daily business to reflect on his Duty ;
and consequently such a one must be a
downright Atheist ; and an Atheist sin-
ning on this side the Law, has nothing
to restrain him but the apprehension of
infamy, and the fear of becoming contemptible.

Besides, a Layman who transgresses,
has his Rector or his Curate to remind
him of his duty. Shall a Clergyman
who is an ill liver go on without admonition. Is that for his advantage, or
the benefit of his flock , or the good
of the publick.

We own indeed that it is our duty
to be instructed by them, yet ought
they sometimes to take their turn,
and be subject to our remonstrances :
As the *Roman* Consuls, if we may have
leave to make such a comparison, were
accountable to the Tribunes of the people, by the policy of that constitution.
Thus I have answer'd what may be objected from Reason against the Stage in
general, and what Mr *Collier* has objected

jected against the *English* Stage in particular, I mean as much as was fit to be
anſwer'd. For there is no defending
the Immodeſty, or Immorality of, or
unneceſſary Prophaneneſs of ſome of
our Plays. Let us now come to the objections which Mr *Collier* has brought
from Authority.

CHAP. III.

The Objections from Authority Anſwer'd..

"THe objections from Authority are
of two ſorts, Councils and Fathers. But now let me ask Mr *Collier*
this queſtion, Were theſe perſons in-
ſpir'd or no ? That is, did the Spirit of
God dictate whatever they writ to 'em ?
If he ſays it did, I have nothing to ſay
to ſuch a man , but abandon him to
Eccleſiaſtical cenſure   If he ſays it did
not, why then I muſt tell him, that we

live

live in an age in which there are persons that are too judicious, and too generous to forego their reasons for meer Human Authority. An age in which we account it not only an absurdity, but a sin to believe in any thing under Heaven; as well knowing that Reason is the top of all human things; and tho not so sacred as Revelation, is in some measure Divine. For Reason is given us by God for our guide, where we have no Revelation to contradict it. And both Human Authority and Revelation hold and depend on Reason. We always assent to Revelations divine Authority, because Reason assures us, that we always ought to assent to it: And we sometimes refuse to acknowledge human Authority, because we are convinc'd by Reason that we ought not to submit to it.

For the Councils he has cited, I must tell him, that we are not oblig'd to acknowledge any of those Councils Infallible; but refuse to be determin'd by their decrees, unless they are confirm'd by Reason or Revelation.

Now I desire to know of Mr *Collier* whether he himself pays the last deference

rence to thofe Councils or no? If he
anfwers, that he owns their Authority,
how durft he appear to have read fo
many Plays as he has cited thro out this
Book, when the Decrees of thefe Councils
even in this very cafe appear from his
own citations fo much ftronger againft
the Clergy than they do againft the
Laity? But if he anfwers, that he dif-
owns their Authority, with what prodigious affurance can he offer to impofe
it on us that while he takes his own fa-
tisfaction he may laugh at our credulity?

But to come to the Fathers, they had
their reafons for crying out againft the
Stage, which cannot fo much as be pretended to be reafon to us. They had
chiefly five, and thofe five reafons will
ferve to anfwer whatever has been cited by Mr *Collier* in his long Ecclefiafti-
cal fcrowl.

Firft, Plays in their time were a part
of the Pagan worfhip; and that in the
beginning of Chriftianity was alone a fuffi-
cient motive to oblige the Fathers to forbid thofe diverfions to the new Chriftians,
feveral of which may be very well fup-
pos'd to be not yet confirm'd in the
Faith.

The

The Second reason why the Fathers forbad the first Christians Plays, was because the Combats of the Gladiators were mingled with those diversions, and something which was full as barbarous.

Media inter Carmina poscunt
Aut ursum aut Pugiles. Hor. ep.1. l. 1.

The Third was the gesticulations of the Pantomimes, which indeed were unsufferably lewd, and unfit to be seen not only by Christians, but by any civil people.

Let any one but consult what Mr *Collier* has cited from the Fathers, and he will find that these were three of the main reasons which prevail'd upon the Fathers to forbid the Christians the diversions of the Theatre.

'Tis not lawful (says *Theophilus*, whom he cites first) *for us to be present at the Prizes of your Gladiators, lest by this means we should be accessary to the Murthers there committed. Neither dare we presume upon the Liberties of your other shews, lest our senses should be touched and disobliged with indecency and prophaneness.*

And *Tertullian*, whom he cites next, says in his Apologetick, *We keep off from your publick shews, because we can't understand derftand the warrant of their original.*

But there are two reafons behind; the firft of which was drawn from the purity of the primitive times. Which makes *Tertullian*, as Mr *Collier* has cited him, cry out, page 354. *But if you can't wait for delight, if you muft be put into prefent poffeffion, &c.* By which *Tertullian* feems to allow, that diverfions indeed are neceffary, but that Chriftians will find abundant entertainment in the very exercife of their Religion. This, I muft confefs, was very well directed by *Tertullian*. But if *Cato* was formerly laugh'd at, for fpeaking in the Senate as if he had liv'd in *Plato's* Republick, whereas he was really in the very dregs of that of *Romulus*, how fhall this upftart Reformer efcape contempt, who has apply'd to this profligate Age, what *Tertullian* directed to thofe fervent Chriftians, whofe Souls were flaming with divine love in the purity of happier times.

Thus have I examin'd four of the five reafons, not one of which can be a reafon to us. For, neither is our Drama a part of Idolatrous worfhip, nor have we either Gladiators or Pantomimes; nor

K 3   will

the people of this age be satisfy'd to be
always entertain'd with the Scripture,
but require other diversions.

But the fifth reason is yet to come;
by which it will appear, that these venerable Gentlemen are by no means quali-
fied to judge of a cause, of which it appears even from Mr *Collier*'s citations,
that they have not the least knowledge.

For, says the Bishop of *Antioch*, whom
he cites first. *The Tragical distractions
of* Tereus *and* Thyestes *are nonsense to
us.* Now could any man possibly talk
thus, who had the least knowledge of
the nature of Tragedy, and particularly
of that Tragedy? It was below that
Prelate to consider *Horace* , for he
would have told him,

> *Iræ Thyesten exitio gravi*
> *Stravere, & eltis urbibus ultimæ*
> *Stetere causæ, cur perirent*
> *Funditus, Imprimeritq; muris*
> *Hostile aratrum exercitus Insolens.*
> *Compesce mentem.*

Is the Moral which the Poet draws
from this Fable nonsense to us? Is it
impertinence in a Poet to tell us, that
we ought to restrain our anger, because
the indulging it has often brought
                                    men

men into fatal calamities? For had this Prelate underſtood this affair, what could he have poſſibly diſlik'd here? The Moral or the Fable? The Moral? That methinks ſhould be hardly becoming of a profeſſor of that Religion, which is therefore extoll'd above all others, becauſe it is more Moral. Was it the Fable then which offended him, or the manner of conveying the Inſtruction? Methinks it is ſomething odd in a Chriſtian Prelate to condemn that method of Teaching which was chiefly practis'd by his great Maſter, whom he profeſſes to imitate.

But now to come to the Author De Spectaculis : *What need I mention, ſays he, the Levities and Impertinence in Comedies, or the Ranting Diſtractions of Tragedy? Were theſe things unconcern'd with Idolatry, Chriſtians ought not to be at them. For, were they not highly criminal, the foolery of them is egregious, and unbecoming the gravity of Believers.*

Now let me ask Mr *Collier,* whether it be lawful for Chriſtians to read Hiſtory? It would certainly be the abſurdeſt thing in the world to deny it. Now

K 4   *Ariſtotle*

Aristotle has declar'd very formally that Tragedy is more grave and more instructive than History. And tho when the question is concerning Grace, I will believe the least of the Fathers before *Aristotle*, and all his Interpreters the Schoolmen together; yet where the dispute is concerning the nature of Writing, and the colours of Speech, I will believe *Aristotle*'s single testimony, before all the Fathers and Councils joyn'd in a body.

Tho Plays are forbidden by the Fathers and Councils, yet the Fathers own, and Mr *Collier* owns, that they are not forbidden by Scripture : Nor are they forbidden by Reason. For who are they who frequent them? Who are they that approve of them? Who are they that have not the least scruple about them? Not a parcel of fools that are carry'd away by meer imagination, and are only fit for *Bedlam* ; but the best and most reasonable part of the Nation, and particularly a thousand whom I could name that are considerable for their extraordinary qualities. Now I cannot for my life apprehend upon what account any thing

thing that is not forbidden **by God ;** that is neither prohibited by Reaſon nor Revelation, ſhould be forbidden by men. We know what our Saviour has ſaid in St *Matthew* of thoſe who teach for Doctrines the Commandments of men, *c.* 15. *v.* 9. That it renders all their zeal ineffectual. But then, ſays *Tertullian*, as he is cited by Mr *Collier*, *p.* 245. *The Play-houſe is implicitly, tho not expreſsly forbid by the Scripture, in the firſt verſe of the firſt Pſalm : Bleſſed is the man who walketh not in the counſel of the ungodly, nor ſtands in the way of ſinners, nor ſits in the ſeat of the ſcorner.* But then ſay we, that nothing can be forbid by this, but what the Scripture or Reaſon have declar'd to be the counſel of the ungodly, and the way of ſinners. Now, as we have manifeſtly ſhown above, neither Reaſon nor Revelation ſays that of the Theatre. And as for the ſeat of the ſcorner, that part of the Text can only be applicable to Comedy, and is full as applicable to the Preſs, and ſometimes to the Pulpit itſelf.

In the next place, ſays the Author *De Spectaculis*, as he is cited by Mr *Collier*,

lier, p. 262. Some have thought the
Play-house no unlawful diversion, because it was not condemn'd by express
Scripture. *Let meer modesty*, says he,
*supply the Holy Text, and let Nature
govern, where Revelation does not
reach. Some things are too black to lye
upon Paper, and are more strongly
forbidden because unmentioned. The
divine wisdom must have had a low
opinion of Christians, if it had descended to particulars in this case. Silence is
sometimes the best method of Authority. To forbid often puts people in mind
of what they should not do. Thus, say
Tertullian,* says Mr *Collier.* But for my
part, I both hope and believe that he
wrongs him. For it is incredible to
me, that a Father of the Church should
reason, in so absurd a manner. For the
chief reason why *Tertullian* affirms that
the frequenting of Plays is not forbid
by Scripture, is because the crime is too
black to be particularly insisted on. As
if St *Paul* in the first Chapter of the
Romans had not descended to particular crimes of a blacker nature than this.
Can we suppose that Scripture, which
is a revelation of the will of God, and

2

a supplement to the law of Nature, should descend to condemn things which Reason had before condemn'd as abominable, and utterly against Nature? and shall it take no notice of things which are allow'd by Reason, and the Law of Nature (as we have shewn that the Theatre is) and which consequently cannot be discover'd to be sins but by the light of Revelations? Could St *Paul* in the 5th Chap. to the 1 Ep. to the *Corinthians* be so particular as to descend to a crime, which, when the Apostle writ the Epistle, concern'd but only one, who had married his Father's Wife, and which could never be suppos'd to concern very many, because the crime was against the custom and consent of Nations: Could the Apostle of the *Gentiles* I say descend to this, and think it too particular to mention a sin which concern'd the salvation of so many thousands who were then alive, and of so many millions who were to succeed them? Nay, could St *Paul*, in the 7th of the 1st Ep. to the *Cor.* descend so particularly, as to give his advice against Marriage, which was neither forbid by Revelation nor Reason, but

was

was highly warranted by both, as absolutely neceſſary for the propagation of Chriſtianity, and the accompliſhment of the promiſes? Could the Apoſtle, I say, deſcend to this, and take no notice of a sin of ſo black and damnable a nature as frequenting the Theatres is by Mr *Collier* pretended to be? A sin too which endanger'd the ſalvation not only of the Chriſtians to whom he writ, but thoſe who were to ſucceed them in all poſterity? But, ſays *Tertullian*, the Apoſtle had no occaſion expreſsly to condemn what is condemn'd by Reaſon. But that which was a reaſon in *Tertullian*'s time does not ſubſiſt in ours, as we have plainly ſhewn above. But if any one at laſt ſhall urge, that the acting of Plays was condemn'd by expreſs Scripture, becauſe it was a part of the Pagan worſhip, and Idolatry was expreſsly condemn'd; to this I anſwer, That nothing can make more for my cauſe than this: For ſince the Spirit of God condemn'd the repreſentation of Plays only as they were included under Idolatry, you muſt either ſhew that the Spirit of God did not foreſee that in proceſs of time they would ceaſe to be Idola-

Idolatrous, which to affirm is horrible
Blasphemy; or you must acknowledge,
that by condemning them only under
the general term of Idolatry, he approv'd them, and allow'd of them, as
soon as they should be no longer Idolatrous; or else you must be forc'd to
acknowledge that the word of God is
defective, and does not contain all
things which are necessary to the salvation of his people. Besides, it may
be manifestly prov'd from St *Paul*, that
the Idolatry of them extended no farther than to the representation of them,
which representation was render'd Idolatrous, only by the direction and intention of the Magistrates and Publick,
at whose expence they were represented; for St *Paul* has sufficiently warranted the writing them, and consequently the reading of them, by citing
a verse of a Comick Poet in the first
Epistle to the *Corinthians* ch. 15. v. 33.
for if those writings had been in themselves Idolatrous, St *Paul* durst neither
have read them while a Jew, nor cited
them while a Christian, Idolatry both
to Jew and Christian being alike abominable. But it is evident that he has
cited

cited them ; for it is known to all the
world , that *evil communication cor-
rupts good manners*, is a verse of *Menander*, and the *Corinthians* particularly
could not be ignorant of it. Since then
the Spirit of God thought fit to put the
verse of a Comick Poet into the mouth
of his greatest Apostle, as very fit for
the instruction of his people, and the
reformation of mankind ; and since the
same Spirit has said not a Syllable to
condemn either Plays or Theatres, any
farther than as they are included under
Idolatry, it seems to be very plain to
me, that he has not only approved, but
recommended Plays to his people, when
they are not corrupt and idolatrous.
For the *Corinthians* saw plainly that
St *Paul* had read *Menander*, they were
convinc'd that he had cited him for their
instruction, and consequently that he
approv'd of him : since then they were
satisfied that the Apostle read him, why
might not they do the like, when St
Paul had not said so much as a word to
discourage 'em. Now if the reading him
could be allowable, why should not
the seeing him be equally lawful, when
the representation should cease to be
corrupt and idolatrous ?   And

And therefore St *Thomas*, and the reft of the School-men, who liv'd when Dramatical reprefentations were no longer Idolatrous, have loudly declared them lawful ; and they are at this very day encouraged in Countries, where they are mortally fevere againft any thing that offends Religion, and where the cruelty of the Inquifition is moft outrageous. Thus have I endeavour'd to fhew, that Plays are inftrumental to human happinefs, to the welfare of Go_ vernment, and the advancement of Pi_ ety ; that Arts and Empire have flou- rifh'd with the Stage, which has been always encouraged by the beft of Men, and by the braveft Nations. After which I hope the Enemies of Plays will be reconciled to our Theatres, and not by perfifting in their averfion , affect to feem more wife than the *Athenians*, more auftere than the *Romans*, more nice than the School-men, more cruel than Inquifitors, and more zealous than the Apoftle of the *Gentiles*.

F I N I S.

ERRATA.

PAge 6: for *that is* r. *it is*, p. 9. f. *these paſſions* r. *the paſſions*, Ib. f. *in theſe a full* r. *in a full*, p. 24. f. *even theſe* r. *even in theſe*, p. 32. f. *action* r. *citation*, p. 38. f. *who liv'd* r. *who was born* p. 44. f. *Stage* r. *State*, p. 54. f. *ſeeing* r. *ſaying*, p. 65. f. *not by* r. *not only by*, p. 70. f. *thoſe opinions* r. *the opinions*, p. 77. f. *verum* r. *rerum*, p. 78. f. *them* r. *it*, p. 80. after *eſpecially* r. *Treaties of a State.*